TEACHING LOW ACHIEVING AND DISADVANTAGED STUDENTS

By

CHARLES H. HARGIS

Department of Special Services Education
The University of Tennessee
Knoxville, Tennessee

Designed for classroom teachers as well as administrators, this volume clearly explains the reasons behind the learning and behavior problems of low achieving and disadvantaged students. It then describes a variety of educational practices intended to help these students, including recommendations for marked changes in educational structure and practices. A sampling of other topics discussed herein includes: the grading system, student-centered curriculum, a new perspective on testing, and major changes in the role of the teacher. Instructional delivery systems based on curriculum-based assessment and cooperative learning are also proposed.

CHARLES C THOMAS • PUBLISHER
Springfield • Illinois • U.S.A.

TEACHING LOW ACHIEVING
AND
DISADVANTAGED STUDENTS

TEACHING LOW ACHIEVING
AND
DISADVANTAGED STUDENTS

By

CHARLES H. HARGIS

Department of Special Services Education
The University of Tennessee
Knoxville, Tennessee

CHARLES C THOMAS • PUBLISHER
Springfield • Illinois • U.S.A.

Published and Distributed Throughout the World by

CHARLES C THOMAS • PUBLISHER
2600 South First Street
Springfield, Illinois 62794-9265

© *1989 by* CHARLES C THOMAS • PUBLISHER

ISBN 0-398-05529-7

Library of Congress Catalog Card Number: 88-23305

With THOMAS BOOKS *careful attention is given to all details of manufacturing
and design. It is the Publisher's desire to present books that are satisfactory as to their
physical qualities and artistic possibilities and appropriate for their particular use.*
THOMAS BOOKS *will be true to those laws of quality that assure a good name
and good will.*

Printed in the United States of America
SC-R-3

Library of Congress Cataloging-in-Publication Data

Hargis, Charles H.
    Teaching low achieving and disadvantaged students / by Charles H.
Hargis.
        p. cm.
    Bibliography: p.
    Includes index.
    ISBN 0-398-05529-7
    1. Underachievers—United States. 2. Socially handicapped
children—Education—United States. I. Title.
LC4691.H37 1989
371.95′6—dc 19   88-23305
                                                                          CIP

PREFACE

My research on the requirements for repetition in learning has led me to emphasize it in my teaching and writing. I have found that the amount of repetition needed to learn something new is seldom appreciated.

Some may find my use of repetition burdensome. Some will find it helpful.

It should be noted, though, that no amount of repetition will help in learning something if the learner is not yet ready to learn it.

C.H.H.

ACKNOWLEDGMENTS

I am indebted to the many teachers who, in their classrooms, have revealed or tested the ideas formulated in this book.

I am thankful to Linda Hargis for all the helpful editing.

CONTENTS

Part Five

TEACHING LOW ACHIEVING
AND
DISADVANTAGED STUDENTS

Chapter 1

CENTRAL CONCERNS

In an open letter to presidential candidates (AP, 1987), David T. Kearns, chairman of Xerox Corporation, charged that America's public schools are turning out a product with "a 50 percent defect rate." The public schools are supplying a work force, one fourth of which have dropped out of school and another quarter that graduate but can barely read their own diplomas.

Mr. Kearns's figures concerning dropouts and low reading achievement are, unfortunately, accurate average estimates for the nation. There are bright spots, but there are some very gloomy ones. We have a big problem. What should be done about it? Mr. Kearns called for a radical restructuring of the schools to change these dismal results.

Further, he said that Xerox expects completely defect-free parts from its suppliers. He claims they get 99.9 percent and are still trying to correct that last tenth of a percent. The press report did not indicate what percent of "defect-free" students Mr. Kearns expects from our schools, but one assumes he meant at least 99.9. Is this too grand an objective?

Explicit in Mr. Kearns open letter is the idea that the "defects" are the result of inadequacies in our schools. Others, however, argue that the defects are caused by outside factors. The television set in the average American home is on for over seven hours a day. The typical school-age child spends more time changing channels than he does reading. Could not this be a cause? Certainly there could be little time for concentrating on homework in such a television-dominated environment. What about single-parent families, or the latch-key children? Too little parental supervision exists. Could this be the cause? What about disadvantaged children? There are some children whose environment is so limited that they lack the enriching experiences necessary for normal achievement in school. Is this a cause? Still other views hold that the defects are part of the children themselves. There is definitely an enormous increase in the number of children being identified as learning disabled. Maybe there is some organic basis for all the problems, some sort of mass dyslexia.

I, frankly, favor Kearns's view that the problem is with the schools. The schools have control of students for about as long as they are in front of television sets. There is enough time during the school day for instruction and for reasonable achievement. Nursery and kindergarten programs can enrich the experience base sufficiently for entry at some place on the curricular ladder. Also, there is increasing evidence that most of the students who are currently being labeled as learning disabled are first and foremost victims of defects in the schools, not in themselves (Hargis, 1987; Gickling and Thompson, 1985; Tucker, 1985). These normal, but low achieving students are called curriculum casualties. This label, "curriculum casualty," is intended to identify the source of the problem which is in the schools, not in the student or his home.

Even for children who are labeled as disadvantaged, I believe the problem is most often one of the schools. Poor white, black, and Hispanic students may have experiential and health deficits, but their achievement shouldn't lag farther and farther behind their potential as they go through school. Typically, it does. Our schools need not permit discrepancies between achievement and potential to emerge in these children. When potential for achievement exists, schools should provide instruction to match that capacity level. Discrepancies between achievement and potential are symptoms of deficiencies in schools (more often than in the student) or in his home.

Schools must accept the responsibility for the problem of discrepancy between achievement and potential for achievement. Students should learn as much as they are able to. Our schools should not shift the blame for this lack of achievement to the student, the home, or to the social condition. Most of the problem is with the schools.

The students who comprise this group of defective products of our schools are the low achieving and disadvantaged portion of the population. However, their defects are not exactly of the kind most people imagine. The ability to learn to their potential is not impaired. The difficulty these students have is more like the problem expressed in these modifications of old clichés: The students are "at the right place at the wrong time," or they are "a day early and a dollar short." Stated more directly, these students don't fit into the structures and standards imposed by the schools. We must remember that the students are not abnormal. We must also remember that normal does not mean average. Normal is a range or distribution. The concepts of normal and average are confused to the great disadvantage of low achieving students.

When normal students present themselves at the door of their first grade classroom, they are not all exactly six-and-one-half years old or exactly 38 inches tall; neither is their readiness for learning exactly the same. All traits, physical or mental, vary remarkably among any group of student, no matter how much the chronological age range is restricted.

Within any narrow age grouping, some students will be remarkably talented in some areas and much less talented in others. Our tolerance of variation in abilities among children is astonishingly mixed. We are quite accepting of variation in musical ability or athletic ability, but we seem very reluctant to accept variation in academic ability. We want children to perform uniformly to the curricular standards provided for their age-appropriate grade.

If children are enormously varied in abilities and readiness character- istics, then it stands to reason that the schools' organization should be sufficiently flexible to comfortably accept them all. However, almost the opposite is true. The curriculum of our schools is laid out in a lock-step sequence.

Emmett Betts (1936) was the first to observe the lock-step nature of school organization and to comment on the effect of this organization on children. The curriculum is laid out in a segmented hierarchy of objec- tives that fit in the kindergarten through twelfth grade school years. A segment of the objectives are sequenced across each nine-month incre- ment that makes up each school year. All students that enter are expected to start at the same point and progress through the same objectives at the same rate. A division in the secondary curriculum is used to separate more academic from less academic students, but the lock-step expecta- tion continues through either track taken.

Here resides the problem of lower achieving children. They may share the chronological age of the students with whom they begin school, but they do not share the same readiness and learning facility to benefit from curricula so rigidly offered. They are a little lost when they start, and, should they happen to get on the curricular track, they can't keep up the pace.

Most children manage to do well in the lock-step organization. The curricular sequences and instructional materials which dominate have emerged over the years to fit the threshold of skills and learning rates of the majority of students. The fact that the majority of children succeed in these curricula gives misleading testimony to their effectiveness for all children. We have the mistaken impression that if so many students manage to succeed, then all students are capable of such success. The fact is, about 15 to 20 percent of students in the primary grades fail (Betts, 1936; Glasser, 1971; Jansky and de Hirsch, 1972), and the high school dropout rate is almost 25 percent. This dropout rate is largely attributable to academic difficulties. These students are not voluntary failures; they are simply outside the threshold of the curriculum.

The fact of failure is so pervasive that we have come to accept it as almost natural. We have even evolved grading systems to both explain and justify failure (Hargis and Terhaar-Yonkers, 1988). Grading systems are based on percentages or normal curve systems. In any given classroom, students will respond to the level of instruction provided in predictable ways. Their performance will follow the pattern of a normal curve. The more able students will get very high marks, the bulk of the students will get passable marks covering the middle range, and the low achievers will receive the poor and failing grades.

Grading systems based on normal distributions have been with us for over sixty years (Cureton, 1971). The 6-22-44-22-6 grading distribution is an accurate representation of what happens to any normally diverse group of students, at any grade level, when they must deal with a single level of instruction. It is sad that we feel obliged to use this grading system. The lock-step curriculum and the grading system have a mutually perpetuating relationship. We need a single level of instructional difficulty in order to produce a distribution of grades, and, in order to induce a distribution of grades, we must give only a single level of instruction.

We are in a constant dilemma; we say we are appalled by high failure rates, but if students only received good grades there would be complaints of grade inflation and lack of standards. The curriculum itself is the cause of the failure, and we are unlikely to modify its form if we hold onto standard grading practices.

Our expectations of achievement for students also contribute to the problem. We expect all students in the same age group to perform within grade level standards. If they don't perform adequately in the grade level work, then it is the students' problem, not the schools. We hold the lock-step curriculum in such unchallenged esteem that we simply assume it is the appropriate way to manage the educational process. Reinforcing the lock-step curriculum is the almost universal use of commercial, instructional materials. Reading, math, language arts, social studies, and science programs dominate and define curricular organization. Shannon (1984) points out that these commercially prepared materials are given enormous credibility. They are essentially reified, a state of grace only a little less than gained by being deified. These materials are lock-step in nature. The lock-step of the curriculum requires and reinforces the use of lock-step materials. Thus, they exist in a mutually reinforcing relationship that conserves and strengthens the existence of both.

These materials are designed to fit the grade levels and calendar sequences of the schools. A level of instructional materials is assigned to each grade. The materials contain and define the curricular objectives, and they are organized in the lock-step. When students fall outside the requirements of the materials assigned, they will be in trouble. If the rate at which the basal program proceeds along the curricular sequence exceeds the rate the student can manage, he falls behind.

Again, so many students use these materials adequately that we are falsely drawn to expect all children to benefit from them. If they do not, then something is wrong with the student. And, after all, weren't these materials and programs designed by "experts?" They were "scientifically" formulated; therefore, the fault for failure must be the students'. We expect all students to perform adequately in such excellent curricula and instructional programs.

We seldom suspect that the schools' curricular organization is responsible for "defects." We may believe that the student must study harder to attain his grade level or to get a passing grade. We may believe that teachers should use more innovative methods to bring the student up to grade level. We think of the "defect" as being the discrepancy between the student's level of function and where he should be in terms of grade placement. The real defect occurs when a discrepancy emerges between a student's potential and his actual level of academic function. If a student's potential is somewhere below his grade level placement, it is fruitless to try to close this kind of gap. Students do not willingly or voluntarily fail. Failure is imposed on them by our practice of making all students work on the grade level assignments and then expecting them all to work fruitfully there.

A condition nearly as negative as failure can occur when academically talented students are required to perform grade level work. Their progress may well be retarded by expecting them to proceed through the same lock-step sequence of curricular objectives as the majority.

As was mentioned earlier, educators tend to attribute poor achievement to the students or their home. The students' failure to learn to grade level standards, they say, is due to learning disabilities, or environmental and cultural disadvantage.

Critics blame the schools for not making the students achieve to grade level standards. They accuse the schools of making the students drop out. They blame the schools for these defects, but their reasoning, if partially accurate, is deficient.

The problems or defects are not really in most of the students; neither is the problem one of lower than grade level achievement. It is a problem of lack of achievement and lack of success. It is brought on by institutionalized, organizational and curricular rigidity, together with the expectation for students which our blind faith in such institutions fosters. The defect really produced is one of achievement lower than the students' potential, and this defect is brought on by the schools.

In past generations, the dropout rate was actually much higher. Our expectations then, however, were not so much on completing school as in merely acquiring basic literacy and computational skill. Many able students dropped out unnoticed and were absorbed into the work force. The passage and enforcement of mandatory attendance laws brought increasing enrollments but also increasing attention to the dropout rate. After all, these laws were intended to keep children in school. Systems of tracking and grouping were devised (Hargis, 1987) to handle the many less academically talented students who were remaining in school. There are, however, limits to the effectiveness of grouping or tracking practices when little attention is given to making the lock-step sufficiently flexible for the extremes in academic ability in the school-age population.

The fundamental changes required to deal with low achievers and disadvantaged students are in the curricular organization, and, since many commercial tests and instructional programs dominate the curriculum, they need attention as well. Additionally, these tests and programs dominate the teaching methodology. They need careful, critical review. These things will receive considered attention in subsequent chapters. However, something else needs careful attention. Failure is the dominating condition of these students. Any attempts to improve their condition must include giving these students the same measure of success that their higher achieving peers experience. Success is fundamental to satisfactory achievement. This concept of a success-based approach to instruction will get equal billing.

Chapter 2

STANDARDS AND NORMS

Standards and standardization have brought innumerable benefits. Standards make life safer and more pleasant and are established for every aspect of life. Religions outline standards for moral or ethical behavior. Professional organizations outline standards of ethical professional behavior. Nations, states, and local governments produce standards and codes that take legal form. Humans have a compelling need to standardize and codify. Standards limit our tendency to anarchy, and they facilitate living together in social arrangements that are increasingly crowded and complex.

Standards extend to all dimensions of our life; most are outside our awareness. A great many affect consumers. Some are legally restrictive codes. Building materials and construction codes are such, though the codes may vary from one locale to the next. Engineering, electronic, and manufacturing associations are all involved in developing standards that affect their respective industries. There are a multitude of such associations. They dictate the number of threads per inch for bolts and screws, the formats of videotape, or the electrical load capacity of a household outlet. Most things we touch in the developed world have been produced or affected by standards.

The Bureau of Standards keeps track of and organizes the myriad standards that are used in measurement and production. Organizations such as Underwriters Laboratory are devoted to testing products to see if they meet standards.

When we switch an audiotape cassette from one tape player to the next, we expect that it will work without a hitch. When we buy a replacement part for an auto we expect it to fit exactly. Interchangeability is an important part of standards. Eli Whitney is credited with developing interchangeability in the manufacturing process. This made mass production possible. So not only does standardization make life more predictable and safe, but it also has immeasurably reduced the cost of many consumer goods and made them widely available. However beneficial standardization may be, it does have its negative effect. The very characteristics that seem appealing may produce serious problems, even handicaps.

The appeal of standardization in the huge enterprise of education is great. Millions of students need to move through the pedagogical manufacturing process. However, we have one problem in education that has been largely resolved in most industries. This problem is one of tolerance. How much variation within the manufacturing process can be managed before defects appear? In manufacturing things, tolerances need be, and can be kept, quite small. This is possible with machine-made parts. Actually, we often think of interchangeable parts as being identical. In fact, they really do vary from each other somewhat. However, if they vary too much, they won't fit. They won't really be interchangeable, or, if they fit poorly, they may cause the machine or device of which it is a component to malfunction. If the items being assembled are all within tolerance, the manufacturing process goes smoothly and the resultant product performs appropriately.

Tolerance defines the amount a part can vary from the absolute and still fit and be made to work. Tolerance limits are measured in miniscule and even microscopic units in industry. Yet, even though the measured differences are small; if a batch of parts were measured on the critical dimensions, the variability of the items in the batch could still be plotted on a normal curve. However, the range of differences would be largely contained within the tolerance limits.

So much for machines. We can control the tolerance measures much better for them than we can for humans. Tolerance limits must be viewed very differently when humans rather than machined parts are concerned. Humans vary greatly on various of their dimensions, but they must fit into a variety of machines and architectural structures, all of which were designed according to some standard. Engineers have done a fairly good job of fitting these devices to humans so that their users can function in and with them adequately. Some common standards are in residential building codes. For example, such codes consider the height and width of door frames, height and depth of stair steps, or the height and depth of counter tops in kitchens. Often, a single measure is the standard for each of these. The standards usually are set at tolerance levels that accept the majority of the normal range of human sizes. For example, the minimum door height for residential doors is set at six feet, eight inches. Clearly, this will be a sufficiently high portal for most individuals. However, consider the range of normal height. I emphasize normal; some adults may be abnormally short or abnormally tall. Some individuals may have an organic basis for their extreme shortness or tallness. Dwarfism or giantism result from genetic defects or biochemical defects that produce height outside the normal range. Probably, the normal range of height, including both sexes, extends from about four feet, six inches to about seven feet, six inches. Obviously, the extremes of the range are unusual and they occur infrequently, but one must remember that these extremes are normal. It is simply their numerical frequency that makes them exceptional.

If these individuals were lined up at the standard residential doorway, most could walk through with ease, and a few more could get through with a little caution. Everyone up to about six feet, six inches could use our doorways without too much fear or inconvenience. About 99 percent of our population can use our doorways without feeling awkward or handicapped. The tolerance limit is generous, but it still excludes a significant, normal portion of the population.

Consider the other end of the height continuum. How do they cope with the standards of kitchen counters and cabinets? Anyone who is shorter than about five feet, three inches has trouble with kitchen cabinets. They simply do not have sufficient reach for items in the upper cabinets, likely even the rear of the first cabinet. When using most furniture, shorter people also have a disadvantage. In most cases they will have difficulty getting their feet to touch the floor without sliding to the front edge of the chair or sofa, thus losing contact with the backrest.

Most people fit adequately within the tolerance levels of most standardized items. However, a significant number don't and they may well experience the inconvenience or discomfort of being out of tolerance on some dimension.

No one has ever suggested, to my knowledge, that if people don't fit the standard, the people be altered in some way so they do. However, it seems quite clear that we expect to alter children to fit the standards imposed by school curricula. A curriculum has been likened to a Procrustean bed (Hargis, 1987). We force and squeeze and try in various ways to make individuals fit, but we only succeed in producing defects. If the students don't fit the tolerance range of the curriculum, they will be failing to achieve and then dropping out. They are casualties of Procrustean methods of dealing with students who are out of tolerance with curriculum standards.

How variable are the students that are in each grade? How much tolerance does the curriculum have for this variability? As it turns out, the students are remarkably variable and the schools have rather limited tolerance.

The primary restriction on variability is the admission-age criteria. The vast majority of school systems have age-of-admission requirements. For beginning kindergarten or first grade, the range of dates (that I am aware of) extends from July to November (Lofthouse, 1987). In other words, some schools require a student to be six years old by July of the year in which he starts school, while others will admit students whose birthday fall as late as November. There is about a four-month range in admission-age requirements. At ages five and six this four-month span can be a significant portion of a child's life in terms of maturation and school readiness.

The earlier the admission age deadline is set, the more generous is the threshold of tolerance. The earlier the admission date, the older and more mature all the students will be. If the earlier date of July first is set, then no student will be less than six years and two months of age when he starts first grade on about September first. He is much more likely to be ready than the youngest child admitted under the latest date, say November first. This child could be only five years, ten months of age. The older the child, the more likely he is to fit into the tolerance limits of the school and the less likely he is to experience failure.

Still, the question of variability in age has not been completely addressed. We have so far only considered the younger end of the range. There will be at least a full year's range in chronological age in the children starting first grade. The older children could be about seven years old when they begin. A year's time can make an enormous difference in the maturity level of children.

If maturity and readiness correlated only with chronological age, teachers probably could handle the differences in their primary-age children. As Spache pointed out (1976), primary grade teachers can manage children who vary as much as six months in academic ability from their grade placement. Actually, readiness correlates rather weakly with chronological age. Other measures of readiness correlate as well or better. Another consideration, then, is that readiness can vary rather independently from chronological age.

Consider a hypothetical first grade class in which all the children had the same birthday and so were exactly six. Also, assume that the children come from identical socioeconomic backgrounds. The students have all been given IQ tests with reasonable assurance that the results are valid since the children are majority representatives of the standardization group. All of the children are in good health and free from any vision and hearing problems. In short, the children are identical with one exception. They vary normally with respect to intelligence. Next, let us restrict the range of intelligence in the group. Let us remove all students whose IQ score falls below 80 and all children whose IQ is above 120. This eliminates any children who by the broadest current definitions could be considered exceptional in IQ terms. There are no children in the class now who could be considered mildly or educably retarded and no children who could be considered academically talented. Transforming the chronological ages of these children into mental ages still produces a very wide range, even with all children being exactly age six.

Consider the children at the extremes. The child with an IQ of 80 will have a mental age of 4.8. The child with the IQ of 120 will have a mental age of 7.2. The range in mental ages in this group is 2.4 years. The mean mental age for the group is exactly 6.0. The lower extreme and the upper extreme are 1.2 years from the mean. Notice that even in this unrealistically homogenous group, the magnitude of variation is double what the typical first grade teacher can handle (Spache, 1976; Hargis, 1982).

The mental age figure is used to indicate the academic readiness of students. Even though various instruments used to measure it are certainly not valid for every child, under the conditions I mentioned above, and with this idealized group, it will accurately reflect the range of readiness. If anyone suspects that any group of kindergarten or first grade children is less variable than my hypothetical group, I would recommend that they ask any kindergarten or first grade teacher about it. Some children entering first grade already can read, while others may only recognize a few letters of the alphabet.

The range of difference is always there, and it is actually far greater than in my hypothetical example. Chronological age will vary by about a year, and this, interacting with mental age of the students, expands the variation in readiness levels. Likely variation in the socioeconomic levels will further expand the range.

One can see that the schools have, at the primary level, tolerance limits of about ± six months. Emphasis should be placed on the minus side. The more academically able students will fare far better. The school work they are engaged in will be very easy, occasionally repetitive and boring, but for the most part comfortable and rewarding. Remember, too, that there are relatively few students at the extremes. The majority of the students will be engaged appropriately with the grade level curricular activities. This gives evidence to everyone that it is appropriate. This observation further makes us tend to think there is something wrong with the students who can't do well. However, for the most part, these students will simply be out of the tolerance limits, and not a part of the majority of students who fit above the minus six months limit (about 80%) and are able to continue from one grade to the next in the lock-step.

Now consider our hypothetical group as they move to the second grade. At chronological age seven, our IQ 80 student has a mental age of 5.6 and our IQ 120 student has a mental age of 8.4. Notice that the range between the extremes has now increased to 2.8 years.

Consider the same students as they begin the third grade. The extremes in mental age at chronological age eight are 6.4 and 9.6, respectively. Notice now that the range is 3.2 years. The range will increase 0.4 of a year each year the group remains in school. Examine our expectations in terms of the curriculum and the students chronological age. The least ready student has an academic readiness age (mental age) of only 4.8 when he starts first grade. He is not really much more than ready for rather unstructured preschool activities. On the other hand, at the other extreme our student has an academic readiness age of 7.2. He has the potential to be reading at the second grade level. In fact, if he comes from an environment where reading is encouraged, he probably is already doing some reading when he starts school.

Our least academically ready student will not reach first grade readiness until sometime between his seventh and eighth birthday. He will have had a difficult time. He has been so out of synchronization with the curriculum that it will be unlikely that he can benefit from the achievement of readiness. He likely has been held back at least once, but even so he will be far outside the tolerance limits of the second grade classroom. School will, indeed, be a very unpleasant place for this student.

At age eight, the readiness age levels of our extreme children are 6.4 and 9.6. The range is now 3.2 years. During this third grade year, the difference in readiness will have increased by a full year from the entry point at first grade. In just two-and-one-half years the range of differences increases by at least a year. The students at the low end have been learning at about a 20 percent slower rate than average, while the student at the upper end will be learning at about a 20 percent faster rate than the average student. This adds to the range in ability year by year.

We can not narrow the normal range of learning abilities by any intervention. I emphasize normal. Various kinds of disadvantage that reduce the students' ability to learn despite higher potential is an entirely different matter. So, when adequate teaching occurs, we can expect the range in achievement to increase rather than narrow. Inadequate teaching may actually narrow the difference, and it does so by permitting a discrepancy between achievement and potential to emerge. Good teaching honors diversity and produces greater differences.

The difference in learning rate and readiness level are a fact in every grade. Yet, as Bloom, Madaus, and Hastings (1981) point out, if in finding where instruction should start and working systematically for mastery at each step along the way, almost any student can learn if one is willing and able to devote sufficient time to the task. Some slower students may make the objective of more difficult academic tasks unreachable given the length of time one can remain in the public schools.

Consider where our hypothetical students will be in terms of readiness when they are fourteen. The slower student has reached 11.2 or about the beginning sixth grade level, and the faster student has reached 16.8 or almost the twelfth grade level. The difference between them has increased to over five-and-one-half years.

One may tend to disbelieve the range of differences within a grade level, but it actually is considerably greater. Academically gifted children are sufficiently common that most teachers will have one or two in their classrooms as a matter of routine. As was mentioned earlier, there usually will be a few children who will be failing, also. Failure precludes most of the achievement to whatever potential a student has. It has been far too common an experience for the author to find children at age eleven, twelve, or thirteen who have made little achievement. All have the potential to learn but are out of the tolerance limits of all their grade placements. They experience chronic failure.

Standardized test data confirm the range of achievement at each grade level. The distribution of scores and grade equivalents show a range of performance that exceeds considerably that described in my illustrative hypothetical group.

The unfortunate circumstances for the slower achieving students is that the tolerance limits of their grade and place on the curriculum do not include them. They are almost never in a position where they can benefit from instruction. As a consequence, their achievement falls continually farther behind their potential.

Chapter 3

THE PROBLEM

Rigid standards that are characteristic of the lock-step curriculum produce complex problems in the schools. Students become casualties of this system and teachers have great difficulty in dealing with them. Researchers and educational specialists devote much of their effort toward "fixing" these students. The problem of students who don't achieve, drop out, or are forced out then confronts the school system and ultimately the community.

Students who are out of tolerance or synchronization with the curriculum have themselves a set of compounding problems. These problems, interacting, tend to increasingly worsen their situation as long as they are in school. The first and most obvious problem is failure. Failure not only marks the lack of achievement, but it has profound emotional effects on the student.

Failure is not reinforcing or motivating; success is. Students who are failing are not only not achieving, they are less and less likely to try. Chronic failure is debilitating. Children who need to be engaged in learning activities are less and less likely to be so occupied. Avoidance of activities that produce failure will be the behavior that emerges in students who experience little success. Instructional activities are viewed as the source of considerable pain and discomfort and, as with any discomforting place in the environment, to be avoided. This is a natural reaction. It is surprising that so natural a reaction brings an even more negative force to bear on such students. Effort may be doubled to keep these students engaged in negative instructional activities. All kinds of motivating strategies have been developed, ranging from ersatz economic systems to corporal punishment. This latter system, of course, truly compounds the students' pain.

The amount of time a student engages in an instructional activity is directly related to achievement. This is usually referred to as academically engaged time or academic learning time. The fundamental relationship between academically engaged time and achievement has long been recognized (Rosenshine and Berliner, 1978; Gickling and Thompson, 1985; Hargis, 1982, 1987). Because of this relationship, we falsely assume that if we can somehow compel a student to stay engaged in an activity, he will learn it regardless of the difficulty of the task. The amounts of time directed to the activity become central to the attempts to improve the achievement of failing children. Such efforts serve only to compound the students' problems and make them more miserable.

When students encounter only failure, they feel increasingly helpless to do anything about it. In the face of continuing failure, the student learns to be helpless. Learned helplessness (Grimes, 1981) is an unfortunate consequence of continued failure. It becomes the primary attitude or approach many children take when confronted with any instructional activity. It is a truly unfortunate outcome of failure experience. The compounded sequence of problems that result from being out of tolerance is failure, lost achievement, learned helplessness.

Children who are given instructional tasks that are outside their skill level cannot devote attention to the task; one cannot continue to merely stare at a task one cannot comprehend. As a consequence of the difficulty to attending, the children who need more time engaged in learning get less and in the process are actually taught the most unproductive approach to the task of learning. The students feel defeated and helpless, and too often they are in circumstances which continually reinforce this feeling.

Chronic failure produces other negative feelings besides helplessness. When students experience very little success, they can not value their work or themselves. These students then will suffer from low self-esteem.

Students come to identify various instructional activities or school in general as the cause of their discomfort or misery. A common reaction to schoolwork and even school is avoidance. Of course, the process of avoidance can bring down still more problems on the students. Truancy and then dropping out are ultimate avoidance strategies.

Depending on the student, the reaction to failure producing instructional activity is varied. The teacher will hope that the student will use the quiet withdrawal strategy. Failure, however, may produce more acting-out or disruptive behavior in children who by nature are more assertive and aggressive. Continued assault on the self-concept of a more naturally aggressive child can cause possibly as much pain and misery to those around him as to himself. Behavior problems are closely associated with academic problems. Far more often, these behavior problems are the result rather than the cause of failure.

Students who find themselves out of tolerance with the curriculum will very likely suffer from what are called Matthew effects (Stanovich, 1986; Hargis et al., 1988). This is, simply stated, "the-rich-get-richer-and-the-poor-get-poorer" phenomenon. Students who are doing poorly in school find that their performance becomes increasingly worse compared to the normally achieving students in their age group.

Not only will all of the problems outlined earlier, such as learned helplessness, lowered self-esteem, and limited time on task, force down the students' performance, but the student will be missing the development of skills along the way. Further, these students will not be getting the normal opportunity for practice. As students move along the curricular sequence and acquire reading skill, they have more and more need and opportunity to practice reading in all subject areas. Students who have not kept pace in developing reading skill find that they cannot do well in the other subject. The other subject areas require increasing amounts of independent reading time. Additionally, the students are missing the added practice in reading that they would otherwise have had. These problems become mutually compounding to the low achieving students. On the other hand, high achievement produces a variety of positive benefits which mutually reinforce still higher achievement.

Low achieving students often find themselves in emotional and academic traps. When rescue attempts are made, they most often seem ineffective. The reason for this is that most efforts at aiding these students are directed at helping them with grade level work. This approach is inevitably doomed, but it remains a persisting approach to dealing with low achieving and disadvantaged students.

The primary problem classroom teachers face is the presence of low achieving students in their classrooms. When students are not doing well in school, most don't just sit placcidly and resign themselves to such a miserable fate. Some do, but a great many are an obvious and disruptive problem that teachers must face daily.

As was mentioned earlier, children that are constantly facing work that they can't do are often off-task and demanding teacher time. Dealing with students who are doing poorly in school is often demoralizing for a teacher. There is nothing so dear to the heart of a teacher as having students on-task, completing their work, and making satisfactory progress. If students do not perform in these desirable patterns (and there are those who don't in every classroom every year), the teachers gradually develop unproductive strategies or attitudes for coping with such students.

I personally feel that "burnout" results from the inability of teachers to cope with low achieving students in their classrooms. When they do try to cope, the strategies used typically do not benefit these students or the teachers.

The pervasive attitude that students must work close to grade level placement colors the approach taken in dealing with them. If the view that the student should work within the tolerance limits is held, then the teacher will likely deal with the out-of-tolerance students as though the problem is the students' responsibility. Students will be getting grade level work to do and getting failing grades. The failing students will either be obtrusively off-task and disruptive or they will quietly withdraw and be entirely unobtrusive, hoping to call no attention to themselves whatsoever. The quiet, withdrawn students are much more likely to survive longer in school (Hallahan and Kauffman, 1986). Their teacher is likely to be indifferent to their lack of achievement. These students are really no problem. The disruptive students will get far more attention. However, the attention will not be directed to the cause of the problem; attention will be directed to the students' behavior. The teacher may try all available strategies and bring all available resources to focus on off-task, disruptive behavior. However, since the cause of the behavioral problems has been ignored, there is limited success in satisfactorily managing it. Then, failing to manage this symptomatic behavior, the teacher wants to rid his classroom of the problem. The low achieving students will be referred to learning disabilities programs, and the disadvantaged students to Chapter 1 programs.

There is some controversy over the effect of the rapid emergence of special education programs, especially those for so-called learning disabled and the compensatory programs, primarily Chapter 1, for disadvantaged children (Mcgill-Franzen, 1987; Gelzheiser, 1987; Pugach and Sapon-Shevin, 1987; Sleeter, 1986). There is some feeling that these programs may have forestalled needed reform in regular education. The fact that the field of learning disabilities evolved, legitimized the belief that there was something wrong with the students and not the system. The existence of these programs is a safety valve for ejecting the most troublesome of students. The net effect is that the tolerance limits for dealing with individual differences remains credible and intact.

Most attempts at dealing with individual differences have concentrated not on the real problem of tolerance but on aptitude. Aptitude here is used in the broadest sense. Sometimes, "learning style" is the term used. Trying to determine a student's strengths as an auditory, visual, or tactual learner has been the focus of considerable research attention and interest. Much effort has been expended in designing instructional activities that capitalize on relative strengths in each of these sensory modalities. As appealing as these notions may have seemed, their effectiveness has proven at the very best to be equivocal. Almost always overlooked is the problem of tolerance or task difficulty.

Much effort, in many directions, has been devoted to remediating academic problems that are believed to be caused by a problem in the student. Such efforts are inevitably futile, except in those minority cases where the problem is in fact in the student rather than in the curriculum.

Inspirational programs have been developed to motivate students to learn. It is as if these students would learn if only they were sufficiently motivated. Almost as clones of the commercial "motivational" workshops that are popular in business and industry, are a similar group of workshops designed to inspire students and teachers. They promote systems that supposedly inspire poorer students to learn and teachers to reach them. Always overlooked is the fact that simply being successful in routine work is the most powerful motivator of all (Forell, 1985; Hargis, 1987).

Educational material in mountainous proportions is commercially produced to reach these problem students. Some of this material does permit some students to experience a little success, but it often is just a diversion of time and effort away from the regular work in the curriculum that the student must perform in and be evaluated in. This special material usually has little resemblance to and no coordination with typical school curricula. The students may use it and appear productive while doing so, but, because it is not drawn from the curriculum, it serves no transitional purpose. There is little or no transfer of skill to help the students who use it perform better in their regular work.

Some researchers study methods of improving the thinking or learning strategies of low achieving students. The assumption that motivates the interest in such methods is that by improving thinking and learning strategies, low achieving students will be able to perform better academically and within the tolerance limits of their chronological age group. These programs may have some merit, though this has yet to be convincingly demonstrated for students who are performing below their actual potential. Nonetheless, such programs perpetuate the assumption that the problem is in the students' brain and not in the curriculum. Low achieving students are always well served if provided instructional activities at their current level of performance and at which they can experience success. This notion may be too obvious and mundane to compete with conceptually more complex and elegant ideas posed by educational researchers, but it is one that sites the problem accurately—in the curriculum, not the student. We should be guided by Occam's razor; the simplest of competing theories is preferred to the more complex.

Over the years there have even been architectural attempts to make schools more tolerant places for students. Open spaces and open classrooms have been tried. However, without changes to make the curricula flexible and tolerant, the changes have been merely physical. Nothing has occurred in the area of learning in regard to low achieving students.

Some administrative experiments have shown promise, but they have not proven to be too durable. The simplest and most promising have been non-graded schools and flexible admission dates and ages. Schools in prisons and correctional facilities have, of necessity, open admission policies because of the transient nature of their students. Failure is difficult to impose if you must provide instruction only where a student is able to start, and there are always new students entering. Glasser (1971) describes the success experienced by students in school in a correctional facility where continued admission of inmates broke down any possibility of lock-step movement.

Administratively, lock-step curricula are convenient to manage. Calendars can be more easily prepared, materials are easy to select and distribute, testing and promotion of students is simple to handle. However, it is this apparent virtue that helps perpetuate the problem of low achieving students. Much of the work in helping these student will be administrative attention to breaking the lock-step.

As was mentioned earlier, special education programs for the learning disabled and Chapter 1 programs have been involved in handling a great many low achieving students. In fact, there is considerable evidence that most of the students being served in programs for the learning disabled are really simply low achieving students. These students have been rejected by the regular classrooms because they couldn't do the work and their behavior became intolerable; the special education program becomes the safety valve. The veritable hemorrhage of students from regular classrooms into programs for the learning disabled is evidence of the rate of rejection. Reynolds, Wang, and Walberg (1987) claim that unless major structural changes are made in regular educational programs, the field of special education is likely to become more a problem and less a solution in providing education for these students.

Whether or not programs for the learning disabled or other mildly handicapped students contribute to the problem in regular education, they do provide a haven for students who can qualify for placement in them. Typically, the academic pressure is relieved immediately, and the student can feel a sense of self-worth and accomplishment by working productively. The negative aspects of labeling the student in order to get the special placement is far less detrimental than the continued failure experienced in the regular classroom. In the special program, the students are more likely to be given work that they can do as a direct matter of course. The frustrating work and the failure which produced the negative and disruptive behavior are no longer there, and these students begin immediately to demonstrate acceptable behavior. Of course, the special educators have done nothing really special for these students, and occasionally they are criticized unfairly for this.

The students who qualify for learning disabilities programs may well be the fortunate ones, however. Unfortunately, they have had to survive failure situations for a sufficient length of time so that a very wide discrepancy between their ability and achievement has developed. Those students who don't qualify typically drop out. The students who have experienced so much failure in the schools will have no confidence in themselves and no love for our institutions. They are very likely to be negative, even damaging, influences in society.

Chapter 4

LOW ACHIEVERS

Low achievement seems a simple notion. In reality, however, the term incorporates a diverse and complex set of notions about why some normal children don't learn as well as others in their age group. The complexity is due to several defective perceptions and logical processes that we have used to explain why some children always achieve less well than their age peers in school. Because we have avoided identifying the curriculum as the source of low achievement, we have never produced a satisfactory idea of the cause or solution to the problem. Each time a new notion about cause or treatment arises, it proves to be inadequate. Consequently, we begin seeking new reasons, definitions, and treatments.

Even the notion of low achievement itself, regardless of cause, suffers from inadequate understanding. What is achievement low in regard to? We tend to think of low achievement as simply a problem of below-average achievement. Part of the problem has to do with how we define average. We tend to think of average as a single number or level like the arithmetic mean. However, average in terms of achievement is not really a single number or level. It is a range of numbers and levels. The lower limit of the average range is the tolerance limit for each grade. Performance below this tolerance limit is usually judged to be low achievement. Let us examine how low achievement can be determined.

The most common way that low achievement is judged is relative to grade level or chronological age norms or averages. If a student's performance is below grade level standards, then he will be considered a low achiever. If the student is not achieving as well as the average student but is within the tolerance limits of the curriculum, he probably wouldn't really be considered a low achiever. For example, if a student were no more than about six months below the performance levels of the other students in his first grade classroom, then the teacher is likely to cope with this difference. If grades are given, this student would be in the D to C grade range. He is just passing; he is getting by.

Now if the student's performance or achievement level is outside the tolerance limits of his grade, greater than the six-month difference in the primary grades, he is very likely failing and getting F's and D's. Failure and failing grades are often the mark of low achievement.

Direct measures of achievement such as curriculum-referenced tests of reading, spelling, math, etc., will give evidence of the level of achievement in the student's own curriculum. Norm-referenced tests of achievement can give indications of achievement, also. The validity of such tests is more suspect (Hargis, 1987, 1982), but they will indicate general achievement with sufficient precision to compare a given student's achievement to that of the other students in his class. These achievement tests yield indexes for comparing students on a normative basis. Percentile rankings or grade level equivalents for scores will show how far from the averages of his classmates or the tolerance limits of his classroom he is. Children who are obviously below could be considered low achievers. Still, many children may not be singled out unless their underachievement is accompanied by some behavior that is annoying to the teacher.

Achieving below grade level does not mean, necessarily, that a student is performing below his potential. Actually, real underachievement can only be gauged by comparing actual achievement with a student's potential for achievement. If a student is performing below grade level but at his potential, he may be considered a low achiever. If the student is also performing below his potential, he might better be classed as an underachiever. He is achieving less well than he has the potential to achieve.

It has been my experience that the vast majority of students who are out of tolerance with the curriculum are underachieving as well. The discrepancy between their achievement and their potential for achievement will be continually increasing as long as they are out of synchronization with the instructional delivery system.

I emphasize that low achievement is often accompanied by underachievement. Relatively few low achieving students manage to maintain an achievement level that matches their potential in the trying circumstances where they normally find themselves. If their achievement level is somehow maintained, it will be because of the intervention of someone outside the school system. Usually, it will be concerned parents who are willing and able to work with their children as tutors and teachers when they see the difficulty with schoolwork that their children are experiencing.

It is indeed unfortunate that even in the few instances where a low achieving student is achieving up to his potential, he will still experience failure in much of his schoolwork. That is, if the best achievement possible for the student is still outside the tolerance limits of his grade and curricular placement.

The children whose low achievement is confounded by underachievement will have their problems still further increased by Matthew effects. The high achiever benefits from them; the low achiever suffers from them. The extreme discrepancy between potential and achievement that emerges over time, as a result, coupled with the helpless attitude toward learning, and the off-task behaviors then demonstrated, often help promote the view that these students are learning disabled. They must have an organic basis for their difficulties. Only neurological impairment could explain such failure to learn given the students' potential for learning. Such judgments dominate our views and definitions of low achievement.

There are, in fact, "real" learning disabled children. However, they are a small minority of the underachieving low achievers.

It is quite important to distinguish real learning disabled students from low achieving students who are actually casualties of intolerant curricula. It is important to distinguish them for the reason that in the curriculum casualty group the problem behaviors are the result of failure, while in real learning disabled children their behaviors will be the primary cause of failure. Real learning disabled children will require special curricula that attend to their problem behavior and learning weakness. These behaviors and deficiencies themselves deserve attention or remediation. Curriculum casualties simply require a straightforward adjustment to the tolerance limits of the curriculum so they can experience the necessary success that puts them on the path of achievement.

Curriculum-based assessment procedures for separating the truly learning disabled from low achievers are described by Hargis (1982, 1987) and will be outlined again in a later chapter.

We have a powerful need to classify, label, and group. When children have problems in achievement, we inevitably try to classify the problem. Almost all systems of classifying students seek to classify, determine etiology, or cause of problem by examining the student. Myriads of tests measuring countless behaviors lead legions of psychologists and psychometrists into the schools to classify children and determine the cause of their problems. Almost assuredly the student can be classified as deficient along some definition (often defined by the test used), or a weakness or skill deficiency can be found within the students. The students so evaluated will be classified or labeled in as many different ways as we have tests or points of view held by the psychometrists.

Theories on the cause of learning problems appear, change somewhat, ebb and flow, but seldom disappear. Like Buridan's ass, we always yield to the theory or label with the strongest attraction of the moment. Changes in funding practice favor one classification system over the other; consequently, more children are given those labels that will give them a chance to benefit from the financial resources.

Possibly, the fortunate children are those who are classified and labeled in one way or the other. Those low achieving students who don't get classified are left to experience failure and most ultimately drop out of school.

As was emphasized earlier in the book, most children who are classified as learning disabled are really, quite simply, low achievers. However, most low achievers are not fortunate enough to get one of the classifications which will provide them haven in special education programs for the mildly handicapped or compensatory programs for the disadvantaged. They are more likely to get non-productive labels, like lazy or unmotivated. Teachers who have these students often wish the students could be labeled and so removed from their classrooms. Ultimately, they remove themselves as they drop through the cracks in our educational system.

Another group of students who have been called disadvantaged are being redefined as learning disabled (McGill-Franzen, 1987). Part of the reason is that socioeconomically disadvantaged students are eligible only for compensatory education, while the learning disabled are eligible for special education. The funding formulas cause school boards to choose the better funded special education programs for both these groups. Most of the disadvantaged students in question could not be considered to be other than low achievers, though their potential for achievement may be artificially low because of experiential deficits, physical or emotional neglect, and a variety of basic health problems.

Compensatory education (Chapter 1) was designed to overcome the effects of poverty. It was based on the assumption that children could catch up if they were given the extra help. The least tractable of the low achieving, disadvantaged group, the ones who fall farther and farther behind, will likely be those redefined or classed as learning disabled. Since low achievement is more common among poor students, they are also disproportionately represented among the learning disabled (McGill-Franzen, 1987).

Low English proficiency is typically a compounding problem when coupled with socioeconomic disadvantage. These students are less likely to be classified as learning disabled and are more likely to receive service in programs which deal with students for which English is a secondary language. Potential for achievement is very difficult to measure in such students. Measures of achievement potential are most often heavily verbal laden and require a student to have normal English language development to be used with any validity.

Children who are failing may be labeled many things. We want to call them something if they are failing. Something must be wrong with them if they can't keep up. We need to diagnose their problem. The result of the diagnosis is the diagnostic label. However, it inevitably sites a problem in the student rather than the curriculum.

The primary point I am attempting to make above is that low achieving and disadvantaged students are overlapping groups and merge again if they are classed as learning disabled.

The procedures for labeling and classifying are remarkably different from one locale to the next. Some students may qualify for special education in one place but not in another. Because of this we cannot discern who is actually learning disabled and who is simply a low achiever. For the students who are not labeled, there may be no successful route through to the completion of school. Those who stay in may do so through social promotion and may not have attained even the rudiments of literacy.

Some students may manage to stay in school and even graduate if there are slow tracks or grouping systems that are organized around curricula based on passing minimal competency or proficiency tests. Proficiency and minimal competency tests can have an important impact on the education of low achieving and disadvantaged students. The issues that their development has raised will be discussed in some detail in a later chapter.

There are a wide variety of classification systems, labels, service systems and specialists who are engaged in serving students who are so organized. Still most low achieving and disadvantaged students are outside their purview. These students fall through the cracks and gaps left between these special programs and services. These students fail and they drop out. These are the students of most concern in this book.

Our system of delivering instruction to these students is terribly inefficient and disjointed. There really is no means of providing much help for them in the educational mainstream as it is structured. There will continue to be pressure to get these students certified as something or other in order to get some kind of help for them. Yet, the very act of providing special programs for low achieving students can be criticized for relieving regular educational programs from engaging in the necessary reforms that would permit these students to be tolerated.

Ultimately, we must not yield to the temptation of labeling these students as handicapped. We should greatly reduce our efforts at finding learning problems in these students. Their learning problem in imposed upon them. The curricular lock-step excludes them from benefiting from placement within the educational mainstream. These students are, or become, curriculum casualties.

Chapter 5

THE CURRICULUM

Curriculum seems an unlikely villain. It is not animate. It would seem benign. It is really only a list of the content and skills that a school plans to teach. How could such a thing be largely responsible for the existence and ailments of low achieving students? Why is it largely responsible for making students drop out of school? Before these questions can be answered, a brief definition will be given of what a curriculum is.

A curriculum is the aggregate of the topics that make up the course of study in a school. The topics may require lengthy developmental treatment as in reading, language arts and math. These courses of study are planned according to a hierarchy of skills. The scope of skills to be taught is laid out in a sequence to be developed. In reading or math, for example, scope and sequence charts are often prepared to cover eight or more school years. Other course work in the curriculum may be placed in the sequence according to the readiness requirements indicated in the curriculum. For example, a course in chemistry requires completion of a considerable amount of math, and so will be placed in the curricular sequence after the necessary math topics have entered the list. The general content and order for most public school curricula are quite similar. The particulars can vary considerably, however.

The reason for some of the differences among curricula has to do with the method of instruction which has been adopted to teach each topic or skill. Methods of instruction should be distinguished from the curriculum, however. Methods of instruction are the mode or medium of presenting curricular topics and engaging the students in instructional activities. The curriculum itself is neutral in regard to method, though commercial instructional materials do supply both curriculum and method.

Method does influence curriculum when it dictates the kind and order of skills to be taught. For example, there are more than a dozen popular reading programs in use. Each of them has a comprehensive word identification skill program that covers several years, beginning in kindergarten or first grade. All of the skills that make up the word identification program are sequenced over the grade levels according to the order in which they will be presented. However, each of these programs emphasize different methods of word identification. Some differences are modest; some are vast. Some present the letter-sound associations for vowels first, while others present the associations for consonants first. Some programs emphasize "phonics" from the beginning, while others may first present a core group of "sight" words from which letter-sound associations are learned. The point is that the skills vary as to which will be presented, how they will be presented, and in what order. The curriculum for each, then, will be different to the extent that their methods vary. Each curriculum can vary in content and order of items, but they all have the same constraints in regard to the calendar. The school calendar has thirteen nine-month years. The kindergarten through twelfth grade pattern has become virtually standard throughout the United States. The only point of variance is in the kindergarten year, which is still not universally available or mandatory in some few parts of the country.

The curriculum, constituted by all of the content areas that make up the courses of study in our schools, must have superimposed over them the school calendar. The scope and sequence of skills and topics must fit within the twelve or thirteen nine-month increments. Only a certain amount of time can be devoted to each topic before moving on to the next. Those assigned to that grade must be covered before the year is over. This must be done in order that the students be ready to continue up the curricular ladder the next year.

Since many of the topics and skills covered in the curriculum are dependent on each other, they must be placed on the curriculum with regard to their readiness relationships. Some skills or topics must be covered before the student can move on to the next. For example, in arithmetic curricula, subtraction and multiplication must be covered before long division. They are required subskills and are basic readiness requirements for long division.

This relationship is not always so direct. Some curricular areas are fairly independent in terms of subject matter. However, most have at least a certain level of reading skill as a fundamental prerequisite. The curricular areas advance in difficulty and complexity as they incorporate previously learned skills.

The areas advance incrementally in difficulty, but they advance in lock-step. More precisely, the grid they form as they are fitted with the school calendar compels students to progress through them in lock-step.

Each school year is further subdivided in smaller units. School systems differ considerably, but generally the divisions are marked by testing and grading periods. The curriculum has giant lock-steps and tiny lock-steps.

At the elementary school level, the curricular items assigned to each small lock-step have been placed there by a normative standard. This placement has been done, not by a formal normative process, but by experience and trial and error over many years. The curricular demands of each level must be reasonable for most of the students in each grade. The level of difficulty and the rate of progression must have a threshold that permits the majority of students to proceed along the curricular path. The threshold of difficulty must be low enough for the majority of students to achieve. As a consequence, it really is well below the threshold of the skill level of the high achieving students. High achievers are required to pace themselves according to the same normative lock-step.

The most direct, if controversial, procedure for dealing with the highest achieving students is acceleration. It is a procedure for breaking the lock-step. Here, the student is permitted to move through the curriculum at an accelerated pace. This includes practices like skipping grades, compressing course work, and "testing out" of courses in which the content has already been mastered. Other options include early graduation and early admission to college or college courses. Accelerated students are helped to increase to their own natural pace through the curriculum. They are not held in the lock-step.

A good approach for the low achieving students would be to permit them to decelerate their pace. Let them move through the curriculum at their own learning rate. However, this approach can be viewed as chaotic, as fostering anarchy. It does not fit students to the curricular grid. Nevertheless, we cannot cure them of their individual differences to make them fit it either.

The normative threshold approach to the curricular pace brings down much criticism on public education, although we may not be aware that this is the reason for the criticism. Since the threshold is set so that the majority of students can progress through, the difficulty level and pace is set low enough that relatively low achieving students can pass. In doing so the instructional activities are below the actual skill level of the higher achieving students. The obvious disparity between the threshold difficulty of the material and the skill of the high achieving students brings down the criticism. There almost always is a significant percentage of high achieving students in the normal distribution of academic abilities that occurs in every classroom and in every school. The fact that the material is too easy, boring, or even babyish for three or four students in each room may obscure the fact that it will be about right for about half the students in the room and will still cause failure in three or four of the lowest achieving students.

The curriculum, unfortunately, is assigned to the grade and calendar sequence and not to individual students. If each student's inherent pace of learning could dictate what curricular item to work on and how much time should be devoted to mastering it, we would not have casualties produced by the lock-step curriculum villain. Curricula should be assigned to students for them to work through at their own pace; curricula should not be assigned to grades, a practice that then enforces the lock-step.

Mandatory attendance laws have compelled many more students to stay in school at least until around age sixteen. As more children stayed in school longer, those stayed who formerly would have dropped along the wayside. School systems, faced with increasing numbers of low achieving students, developed systems of grouping and tracking to deal with the low achievers. Tracking systems routed students with different levels of academic talent through school on different curricular paths. These tracks became noticeably different at the secondary level, especially in large comprehensive high schools where completely different curricula were started to separate the academic or college bound from the various terminal or vocational students. In larger comprehensive school systems the tracking programs could be quite complex. The smaller the school system, the less complex the tracking could be.

This form of "ability" grouping extended into the classroom at the primary and elementary grades. Two, three, or more reading groups are often formed to place children with approximate skill levels together for instructional purposes. However, even with the attempts to find a place for everyone, the tracks and groups remained lock-step or bound by the lock-step.

Grouping and tracking procedures did manage to increase greatly the number of students who completed public school. We forget, or were not there to observe, the much higher attrition rates of the generations preceding the current time.

Grouping and tracking practices reach about as many students as possible given the lock-step organization they serve. They are intended to help fit students into the grids and structures of curricula. Still, about three or four students in each grade at the elementary level are failing, even more are doing quite poorly, and about 25 percent of high school students drop out.

Forcing students into slots produces casualties. There will always be some students who are out of tolerance with their slot. We must restrain ourselves from fitting students to curricular structures by making more structures. Curricula must be assigned to individual students, not students to curricular slots. Much more will be presented on this in subsequent chapters.

There are several powerful influences that conserve the lock-step nature of the curriculum. Its long history is one. It is truly institutionalized in form. It developed in form with the notion that students would stay in the lock-step as long as they could benefit, and then it was expected that they would leave school when they could no longer benefit or participate. Earlier in this century it was quite generally assumed that there was little point in staying in school once a person had learned to read, write and do simple arithmetic. The higher levels of the schools were designed for the incrementally fewer academically oriented students who would remain. Commercial curricula emerged to assist students who were headed to clerical jobs in business and commerce. Other vocational training such as in skilled crafts was largely handled outside of school through apprenticeships. Students who sought these careers quite often left school to seek training on the job. It had become perfectly appropriate to fit students to the curriculum. They should leave when they no longer fit.

Mandatory attendance laws changed things drastically. Schools were compelled to develop less academic curricula and tracks. Vocational offerings expanded. Special education programs for the "educable" mentally retarded served increasingly greater numbers of students, but they were served within the existing lock-step structure that was firmly entrenched.

Another powerful influence that preserves and reinforces the lock-step curriculum is the commercial instructional materials industry. Commercial instructional materials are designed to fit existing curricular structures. If they didn't fit, they wouldn't sell. They fit the existing structure, but, in doing so, they preserve and further institutionalize the system.

Developmental reading, spelling, language arts, and arithmetic programs dominate the three R's curricula. These programs fit the curricula and in fact they are the curricula. As well as providing the day-to-day instructional activities for each curricular objective, they lay out what all the objectives are in a detailed and comprehensive way.

The materials consist of textbooks and seat work activities like worksheets and workbooks for the students. There are manuals and teachers' editions of the textbooks that guide the teacher through every lesson. Tests of mastery are provided at each step. The commercial material fills the time devoted to its subject matter each day throughout the school year. The programs can guide the teacher through each minute of instructional time.

This aspect of commercially prepared material is very appealing. The materials actually provide the lesson plans and instructional activities for the teacher. We have become so dependent on commercial programs that teaching probably couldn't go on without it. We invest almost complete credibility in the validity of these programs. Apparently, we think their creators are omniscient. If we happen to be somewhat dissatisfied with the program we use, we simply look for another one.

The fact is that most of this material is fairly effective. After all, most children make reasonable progress through schools and these programs dominate instruction. The other fact, however, is that these instructional programs are lock-step. These programs provide the tolerance limits. If a student entering a grade has a readiness level below that required to use the material, he will be in a failure situation. Students who are below the readiness threshold quickly lose motivation and go off-task.

These materials provide the pace of instruction. New words are introduced gradually in the basal readers. If the rate of introduction and amount of repetition exceeds the threshold requirements for low achieving students, they cannot benefit (Hargis, 1987, 1982).

Most students can tolerate the addition of a new word about every sixty words (Gates, 1930). However, the words introduced must receive sufficient reinforcement and repetition so they do not remain unknown. Without repetition, they remain like new words. The range of word repetition requirements for our hypothetical class of normal students will be from as few as twenty to as many as fifty (Gates, 1930; Hargis, 1982, 1987; Hargis et al., 1988). Keep in mind that these are averages; all words don't require the same amount of repetition. Some take more, some less; but the average figures show the marked difference in need for reinforcement and repetition among children. The introduction rate in the basal reading programs is fine for most students, and so apparently are the repetition rates for most students. However, actual tabulation of the repetition of each word in the popular basal readers at first grade level shows that none came close to the needed repetition for slower than average students.

The same problem exists in math instruction. The introduction rate and the needed trials to mastery for even basic computational facts are insufficient for below-average students. However, these students must keep pace with the other students. They must keep pace or they will not be ready to take the next lock-step into the following grade.

After the primary grades when most students can begin using reading as a tool or study skill, subject areas become dominated by textbooks. Reading skill is used as an independent means of learning and studying specific subject matter. Science, social studies, health, all subject areas from simple to advanced, are dominated by a textbook. The same textbook is used for all the students in a given course. This is the tyranny of the textbook. One level of difficulty or readability is imposed on all the students. The students must have sufficient reading ability to read the book in order to have access to the subject matter of the content area. If the book has the readability of the average reader in that grade level, then a large percentage of the students will not be able to read it well enough to gain much from it. Textbooks assigned to subjects in the curriculum help form steps in the lock-step.

If students don't keep pace, it must be their fault. The programs are excellent. Most children do well in them; therefore, all children should. If the student does not keep pace, he will be retained. He must repeat a lock-step in its entirety. So goes the lock-step, rigidly moving students, occasionally in reverse. The commercial materials which form the substance and the form of the curriculum are a culpable partner in producing the problems of low achieving students.

Teachers themselves are located in lock-step positions. They train and identify themselves according to grade levels and content areas. The teachers' skills and experience soon focus on a calendar year or years in the curriculum. Elementary teachers fit themselves to their grades and the sequence of skills and topics assigned to it. The teacher becomes the proprieter of a set of curricular objectives assigned to his grade level. The teacher presents this sequence to the students each year, over and over.

Secondary teachers may be responsible for several sections of the same class each year with one or two content areas, for example, two levels of math, two sections of each. The same sequences are presented each time they are taught. They are steps in the lock-step.

Secondary teachers can feel quite bound by their curricular domains. They present the same material in the same sequence year in and year out. That is their job. It is difficult for them to do otherwise since they may see five classes a day, each made up of a new group of students. It would be exceedingly difficult for them to do more than present the curriculum uniformly and give grades, under the pressure of such numbers of students. Teachers assigned to steps in the curriculum also serve to maintain the lock-step.

Chapter 6

TESTS

Tests are regarded with at least as much respect and credibility as the commercial, curricular programs previously discussed. If we are dissatisfied with the results or information supplied by a test, we may seek another, but we won't abandon testing.

There are many good reasons for using different tests and for testing. However, there are some tests and testing practices that are genuinely bad when they are applied to low-achieving and disadvantaged students. First consider some common forms of tests.

Norm-Referenced Tests

The most publicized of the tests used in our schools are the standardized achievement tests. They are also called norm-referenced tests. These tests are used by schools to check student progress and·to check the performance or quality of instructional practice. The results of such tests may also be used by critics of the schools to show how poor the performance of our educational system is.

Standardized or norm-referenced tests are standardized by administering them to groups of students who are representative of those for whom the test is ultimately intended. The standardization sample should be large enough and contain enough students who are sufficiently similar to the ultimate users so that it can give an accurate picture of how this kind of student is performing relative to others in this group. Widely used tests may have very large standardization samples. These tests will have large national representation as well as substantial regional, urban and rural, ethnic, and socioeconomic samples. So, for example, if you want to compare the performance of the poor, white students in your rural elementary school, you probably can find a test that has standardization data on students like yours. Information like this is helpful. The academic performance of these students might look very bad if simply compared to the national or regional norms, but their test results might be viewed more favorably when compared with other students from similar circumstances.

Norm-referenced tests are useful in making a variety of comparisons. A student or group of students' performance can be compared to others like them to evaluate the effectiveness of a school's instructional activities. Students' performance can be checked against their own previous performance to see how much progress has been made. This kind of check is helpful in evaluating new materials or instructional activities. It is also useful, though controversial, in teacher evaluation. How much progress, relative to their own starting place, did students make while under a teacher's care. This is an important measure of accountability.

Norm-referenced tests are used to identify and label handicapped students. Norm-referenced tests, like individual intelligence tests and achievement tests, are used to see if there is a significant discrepancy between potential (usually IQ score) and achievement level. The measurement of discrepancy is a widely used procedure for identifying learning disabled children. Discrepancy between achievement and potential has come to be used more and more frequently, because other means of identifying a learning disability have proven to be unreliable. Since academic problems are the unifying or common feature of all children with learning disabilities, it makes sense to use an academic measure in their identification. Also, and most certainly, there is no reason to identify a child as learning disabled if he is learning as well as he can.

Discrepancy measurement is not without controversy, however. Some of the controversy arises because of differences in the procedures for determining what constitutes a "significant" discrepancy. More significant, to my mind, is the fact that a discrepancy is required in order to be classified as learning disabled. If a discrepancy must appear in order to get help, it means that a student must fail to achieve for a sufficient period of time before a discrepancy emerges. The use of this system basically legitimizes the lock-step; it makes it alright to fail a child. Virtually all low achieving students who come to be classified as learning disabled are identified in this manner. They make up the bulk of the students who are currently classified as learning disabled. This discrepancy is really a measure of their underachievement, not an indication of a learning disability. For some low achieving students, the magnitude of their underachievement is sufficient to qualify them as learning disabled.

Norm-referenced tests give considerable information about the variability of the students for whom they are standardized for. It is a pity we don't take to heart this information. The normative data gives primary evidence of the dispersion of academic ability in each age and grade level. We tend to think of the average performance for the grade level as the arithmetic mean rather than the range covered by a normal curve.

For example, the reported range of raw scores in mathematics for each primary grade on a popular achievement test is 8–41, 9–49, and 14–61. The mean raw score for each of these grades is 19.5, 29.2, and 37.5, respectively. The mean scores change by about eight to ten points from one grade to the next. Notice, however, that there is considerable overlap of scores between each grade level. This same overlap is observable in scores for any subject area. It is normal to have measured performance more than a grade level below and a grade level above the mean for the grade. However, we have the rigid notion that normal includes only the segment above the mean to just below it.

Norm-referenced readiness tests also show the wide variation in academic readiness that exists in any group of kindergarten-age children. Readiness tests have been criticized for their imprecision in predicting specific levels of achievement. However, they are quite good in identifying children who are unready for academic work. Those children who perform in the lower quartile on good quality readiness tests will almost invariably have trouble in first grade.

Readiness tests have a potentially important function, if the information from the tests is acted upon. They give information that can prevent a child from being placed in a situation where failure is likely. Heading off failure is an important test function. There are a substantial number of readiness tests of acceptable quality that can be used for heading off failure. It should be noted that readiness tests do have a tendency to underreferral. They will miss some children who are going to have some problems (Hargis, 1982). Readiness tests can identify about 80 percent of the children who are headed for trouble. They will miss the others because they do not assess factors such as a child's health, emotional state, or conditions in his environment that might also contribute to poor achievement.

Diagnostic Tests

Low achieving and disadvantaged students are much more likely to be tested than the average student and then be adversely affected by the results. Consider diagnostic tests.

There are many diagnostic tests, particularly for reading. When children are performing below the tolerance limits of their classrooms, they are likely to get a diagnostic test to see what their problem is.

Herein resides the first problem with diagnostic tests. The assumption behind their use is that something is wrong with the child. They misdirect our attention from the primary cause of most problems, unsuitable matches between student ability and curriculum difficulty. When diagnostic tests are given, they will invariably show skill deficits in students. Are the deficits revealed by diagnostic tests really significant? This question should be asked far more often. To answer the question one must first review the skills being assessed by the diagnostic test. Next, the skills on the test should be compared to those the student has actually been exposed to in his curriculum. Are they the same skills?

In Chapter 5, "The Curriculum," I described the differences among the scope and sequence of skills that make up the various reading curricula. The same differences exist among various diagnostic reading tests. The skills assessed on a diagnostic test may bear little resemblance to those presented in the curriculum a child is in. If such a test is given, then the student will invariably do poorly. The student will show many skill deficiencies. However, are they "real" skill deficiencies? If the student has never been exposed to these skills, can they be called valid deficiencies?

The answer should obviously be no; however, this is not often the case. Tests are vested with remarkable credibility. We assume they are valid measures, but diagnostic tests are not likely to have the most important type of validity. This is content validity. Simply stated, to have content validity, a test should be made up of the skills the subject is supposed to be measured on. In the case of reading, the skills a subject is being measured on are those on his curriculum. So, in order for a diagnostic test to be valid, to have content validity, it must be curriculum-referenced. The skills tested should be those we want the student to have acquired: those on the curriculum. Unfortunately, few diagnostic tests have or are selected for this quality.

What are the consequences of giving content-invalid diagnostic tests to low achieving and disadvantaged students? If the results of the tests are not ignored, several things may happen. The skill deficits revealed will be viewed as the cause of the students' low achievement in reading. An instructional effort will then be undertaken to remediate the skill deficiencies identified on the test. An instructional program, a new curriculum in other words, made up of deficient skills, will be planned and implemented.

A problem with such an approach is that another curriculum is generated. Instructional time will be devoted to teaching this different curriculum. This will be time taken at the expense of instruction in regular curricular areas. It can be confusing; the student may be getting different skills instruction and all of these activities will have missed the point. The student's problems arose because the difficulty level of curriculum and instruction was too great for his readiness level. The problem was not a subskill deficiency that was keeping him from achieving to grade level standards.

Even if the diagnostic test has content validity, they focus on deficiency. Their purpose is to find something wrong. Inevitably, when giving diagnostic tests to low achieving students, one will find many and varied deficiencies—whatever the diagnostic test measures. Since the automatic reaction to finding deficiencies is to teach to them or remediate them, we can create a very trying situation for a student. This is the diagnostic test trap that we often fall into. The prescribed remedial activities will be made up of things guaranteed unknown to the student. Such focus on weakness often causes extreme frustration in students. Diagnostic-prescriptive activities often maximize difficulty. Teachers often wonder why so little progress occurs after such procedures are conducted!

As was mentioned earlier, a pitfall in the use of diagnostic tests has to do with content validity. Suppose a diagnostic reading test is given to a low achieving student. The student demonstrates a lack of a good number of the word identification skills tested. We then assume that the student's low achievement is the result of the deficiency in these subskills. The deficiency will be in our reasoning, not in the student. Does the test used have content validity? Is the test made up of skills that are in the reading curriculum the student is using. The student may have missed the items because they are not a part of his curriculum or they simply have not as yet been presented.

The test has no content validity. The skills measured are not aligned with or a part of the actual curriculum in use. In these cases, results of diagnostic tests provide trivial or misleading evidence. However, since these tests have so much credibility, their results are likely to be acted upon. This will further divert and dilute attention from the real curricular needs of the student.

When attempting to diagnose subskill deficiency in a student, the diagnostic instrument should be measuring those subskills that are a part of the curriculum the student is using. The remedial effort that is undertaken based on this assessment should be aimed at those skill deficits that are on the curriculum in order to progress further along its path.

The adage that has emerged in curriculum-based assessment (Hargis, 1987) is "choose your tests well for they tend to become your curriculum." Remember, tests are vested with authority. When children are doing poorly, we want to find a reason. Our first reaction is to "diagnose" a student's problem. There are a wide variety of theories as to reasons for learning problems, most of which have nothing to do with a student's curriculum. There are as many tests as there are theories. The person administering the test, i.e. teacher, school psychologist, reading specialist, special teacher, etc., will have their theories and their tests. When the tests are given, the results are treated with respect. The specialist will recommend or implement a program of instruction to deal with the weaknesses or deficits revealed by their tests. The tests, in effect, have dictated a new curriculum.

If the diagnostic test has content validity, (that is, it relates clearly to curricular goals), then no new curriculum is formed. Tests such as these would be said to be curriculum-referenced. People who use "diagnostic" tests should carefully consider the content validity or curricular relevance of the tests they give. If they don't, the instructional programs prescribed will have no more validity than the tests that generate the prescription.

Such tests also divert attention away from the cause of most problems. The deficits sought out are in the student. The cause of problems identified are thought to be in the student. We then further confirm to ourselves that the learning problem is in the student, not in the curriculum or the school.

Basic Skills and Proficiency Tests

"Back-to-the-basics" movements have provided the impetus for the widespread use of tests that measure "minimal competencies" or "basic skills." Lists of curricular objectives are prepared that assumedly represent the minimal academic competencies or skills that all students should have.

What constitutes minimal competency is a somewhat subjective matter. Some lists of competencies have a "life skill" emphasis and so contain more practical items. Some lists are largely academic. Regardless of which bent the minimal competency list takes, they constitute curricula and tests.

Passing these tests is becoming a common requirement for high school graduation. This makes these tests very important to low achieving students. They can become a substantial obstacle to them. They become so important that the tests often form the framework for curricula used with students who will likely have trouble passing them. This is an eminently sensible thing to do when tests become so important. Teachers should teach to the test. Certainly, if the test contains objectives that are so valued by society, they should be specifically taught anyway.

The problem that arises when proficiency or competency tests provide the curriculum which will be used is that this additional curriculum may be at odds with the curriculum already in place. The low achieving student may find himself coping with two different curricula. On the one hand, he may be given the curriculum designed to help him pass the proficiency test, and on the other he may be given the regular curriculum of the school and be graded on his performance in it.

If the school system has made some effort to coordinate the curricular objectives so that there are not significant differences, the two can work harmoniously and to the low achieving students' advantage. However, in most cases the reverse will be true, and the low achieving students will be faced with contradictory forces and a dilution of instructional effort.

Despite what critics say about these tests, proficiency tests have opened new opportunity to low achieving and disadvantaged students. Since passing these tests is a primary criterion for high school graduation, they help increasing numbers of students meet the rather more attainable standards of achievement required. This opportunity will be a true one if the tests do outline the actual curriculum that these students will follow. If the objectives measured in these tests are important, then they are important enough to honor with a basic skill curriculum designed to teach them. If, however, the students are measured with one test but required to work in and be graded on performance in an unrelated curriculum, the opportunity is lost and the dropout rate will continue.

Assessment is important in the effective education of low achieving and disadvantaged students. Current assessment practices usually only make things worse for these children, so current assessment practices must be changed. Assessment must be used to insure the students' success.

Chapter 7

GRADES

W e have a powerful need to grade. Things with the same position, standing, characteristics, or value are grouped together. Oranges, apples, and eggs are graded according to size, color and quality, and they, like children, are given letter grades.

Grades are an institutional part of American education. Grades are used to divide the curriculum, and a grade is a stage in the curriculum. It is also a year's work. The typical curriculum is ordered in a sequence of thirteen grades.

The dominating attribute used for grading students is chronological age. Students who have birth dates within certain boundaries are placed in the same grade. Once in their assigned grade, their performance relative to other students is further graded. They may be assigned to one of several reading groups, depending on their performance in reading. Their relative performance in the group is also graded. The most usual procedure for grading performance is with letter grades.

In spite of our best efforts at grouping and grading students into increasingly homogenous units, variation within each grade or group will persist. Direct evidence of this is provided by the distribution of letter grades that is produced by the students within each of the grades or groupings.

For example, if we check the scores on the weekly spelling test in any elementary classroom, it would surprise no one to see a wide range of scores and resulting grades. The same range would be found if we checked other tests or assignments that are routinely given. The fortunate students get the A's; the unfortunate ones get the D's and F's.

We expect our grouping and grading practices to solve all problems with variability of academic aptitude. However, the distribution of grades that is produced when an instructional task is given to a group of students always confirms the continued existence of variability.

47

Occasionally, we find ourselves in two contradictory positions simultaneously. We want all students to do well, while at the same time we want to have rigor in our grading system. We must maintain standards; we have to be tough. These opposing positions produce a dilemma not easily resolved when we blindly accept the institution of grading.

The underlying reason for the distribution of grades is that one level of instruction is given. The variability in grades is simply indicative of the variability, the individual differences, in learning ability and readiness of the students who undergo the instruction.

Academic ability exists on a continuum. It does not lend itself too well to grouping and tracking practices. Grouping and tracking are used to narrow the range of differences so that one level of instruction can be directed to each group. But there remain students at the high and low ends of the ability range, and they are out of tolerance with the level of instruction offered. Better to find the level of instruction too easy than too difficult, but either position is not the optimal one for either the high or low achievers in any group.

Students in the extremes often share more learning and aptitude characteristics with students in groups or grades below or above them. Even if action is taken to move the student through either retention or acceleration, the movement is usually done at the end or beginning of the year, the year being the grade's time unit. Consequently, acceleration or retention is done in the curricular lock-step.

Perhaps a concrete illustration using chronological age is in order. Children begin the first grade of the lock-step curriculum if their sixth birth date falls before some arbitrarily selected date at the beginning of the school year. They then are supposed to move through the grades with students who became age six between the twelve-month period prior to this cutoff date, even though this supposedly keeps the students with their age-mates. The younger students in each grade will be closer in age to the older students in the grade below than they are to most of the students in their own grade. Conversely, the older students in any grade will be closer to the younger students in the grade above.

The same condition exists for academic ability as for chronological age. The low achieving students are closer in ability to the students in the grade below, and the high achieving students are closer to students in grades above. The differences in academic ability are much greater than differences in chronological age. As was mentioned in an earlier chapter, the range of academic ability in almost any first grade classroom is at least 2.4 years. Chronological age range is only twelve months, but the range of academic ability in the same students is over twenty-eight months! The range in chronological age will stay the same as a group of students moves up the curricular ladder. However, the range in academic ability actually increases and will about double by the time the students are in high school.

Grouping by grades and tracking are efficient means of dealing with a majority of students but ineffective as methods of dealing with extremes in individual academic differences. Why do we impose this practice on all students? It is administratively easier. A majority of the students are able to achieve adequately in the system, so we have deluded ourselves into believing it is appropriate for all students. The grade is the standard of performance and the level by which achievement is gauged.

Performance relative to grade placement is indicated by letter grades based on percentage scores or by letter grades based on a curve. Sixty years ago, the grading systems based on curves were introduced (Cureton, 1971). The most common is the 6-22-44-22-6 curve. The six at either end corresponds to the number of F's and A's. The twenty-two's are the number of D's and B's, and the forty-four represents the number of C's.

Most teachers don't adhere to this distribution when assigning grades. After all, as Glasser (1971) pointed out, each semester three or four students will fail in virtually every classroom of about thirty students. This means that about 12 percent fail. Percentage grading systems are apparently much more severe than grading systems based on curves.

Letter-grade distributions are simply a reflection of the difference in academic skill and achievement that exist in every classroom, given one level of instruction. We should know beforehand that if we give instructional tasks with one level of difficulty to a group of students whose ability varies over many levels, we will get a distribution of grades. If we already know this beforehand, why do we even bother giving grades?

One reason we give grades may be that we feel the need to classify (grade) children. We want to know which of the children are the most and least able. Grades are, in a sense, the primary diagnostic tool. Children who continually get poor grades are identified for further assessment to see if they can be classified as learning disabled. The first step in the diagnostic process is virtually always failing grades.

One fact that should be noted from the use of grades is the distribution of grades is directly tied to the range of levels of instruction being provided. One level of instruction at grade level will produce a wide distribution of grades resembling a normal curve. This will be true if the students in the class are typical. This distribution of grades is primary evidence that individual differences among the students in the class are being ignored. The teacher is strictly adhering to grade level instruction.

A teacher might attempt to provide instruction at a level that was within the threshold of ability of all of the students in his or her classroom. This would still be one level of instruction, but it would be easy enough for even the slowest students to manage. The distribution of scores and grades now would be heavily skewed toward the "A" end. This would be fine for the slow students, but it would be disastrous for the more able ones.

A teacher might attempt to provide a level of instruction to be appropriately challenging for the more able students in the room. The distribution of scores and grades now will be skewed toward the "F" end of the curve. This would be fine for the most able students but disastrous for the rest. The use of a single level of instruction always has negative effects for some students.

The grading system itself perpetuates the use of single level instruction. We think we must give grades, and we think we must give a complete distribution of grades. We can't give all students high grades. That is what grade inflation is. The simplest way, then, to make sure that we get the necessary distribution of grades is to give a single level of instruction that will induce the necessary variation in performance to which we can easily assign grades.

Having a grading system legitimizes giving failing grades. We have a grading system that includes F's and D's. We must maintain standards. We must avoid grade inflation. As a consequence of all these reasons, we must give the failing grades. The only way we can give enough students failing grades is by giving them work that they will fail at doing. The simplest way to do this is to provide only grade level instruction. The grades, themselves, thereby legitimize both failing grades and single level instruction.

Since we assume that everyone should only work at one level, all our attempts at individualizing instruction, remediation, or motivation are directed at trying to make students work up to grade level. Our notion of individualizing instruction is perverted by the system. Many think that individualized instruction is simply individual attention, one-to-one tutoring, or working with small groups. We do not consider the fact that individualization of instruction must, for the most part, be directed at providing instructional activities of appropriate difficulty to students. Classrooms using truly individualized instruction will have multilevels of instruction. Levels of difficulty will match every student's academic ability.

In classrooms where there is truly individualized instruction, no distribution of grades can result. The only way progress can be gauged is through direct observation of what specific skills the student is working on, the amount of progress or achievement on these skills over time, or comparison to grade peers of skills attained on the curricular sequence. Individualized instruction produces acceptable (not poor or failing) performance in each student. Levels of instruction are provided for each student that are doable, not frustratingly difficult. Instructional level activities by definition produce scores that are indicative of comprehension and learning. The high performance necessary for this cannot possibly be assigned a failing grade.

Possibly the most destructive consequence of using grades is that poor performance is blamed on the student. If a student is failing, it is because the student has a problem that is preventing him from achieving to grade level. It is expected that some students will fail. It is not the fault of the curriculum that low achieving students fail; it is their fault. The fact that we have grading curves and letter grades leads us to believe that it is appropriate and even desirable for some students to be failing.

Having grades perverts the use of assessment. Tests are a routine part of school activities. The problem is they are used primarily to give grades. Informal tests are given periodically. Also, any instructional activity that is scored or graded is a form of assessment. When teachers evaluate the work the students do, it is primarily for the purpose of determining a grade. Only secondarily does the evaluation suggest a change in instructional activity. The results of this scoring are noted in a grade book, and the cumulative results produce a final grade.

Assessment should be used primarily for evaluating the quality of the match between the student and the instructional activity being used. Poor scores or grades mean a poor match is made and an adjustment in the instructional procedure or materials is in order. Assessment should be used to assess strengths and weakness in the instructional process, not in the student. Grades cause us to shift the focus completely.

Most assessment only provides a passive reflection of how students perform on a level of instruction. Assessment should be an active component of instruction to be used to monitor the match between student and instruction. Assessment should be used to provide the level of instruction for each student that produces achievement and success. However, since we are bound by the need to assign grades, assessment has become a passive, instructionally useless, activity.

Grades, not achievement, have become the objective. This may not have been intentional, but it is the net effect of using grades. We push students to work harder to improve performance on grade level work in order to get better grades. We should be pushing the curriculum around to fit the students to permit them to work fruitfully at their own instructional level.

Despite awareness of the negative features of grades that have been cited so far, there are individuals who still hold the view that grades have an important function. They should be used to motivate students. Poor grades should be used to make students do better. I will grant that a poor grade can nudge some students to better performance. However, this can only be done if the student is in fact capable of a higher level of performance. In other words, there is a negative discrepancy between the grade he is receiving and the grade normally assigned to students in his portion of the ability distribution. He is already capable of getting better grades, so a poor grade may cause him to improve his performance.

Such a practice will, however, not be motivating for low achieving students; certainly not if there is a discrepancy between his ability and the work he is being required to do. Poor grades will not motivate these students. Poor grades will demoralize them. Chronic failure produces and magnifies a variety of behavioral difficulties that have a very negative effect on a student's motivation.

The grades that are motivating are good grades (Evans, 1976). Consequently, the only students who are motivated by grades are students who are already getting good grades.

Chronic failure is not productive. As Glasser (1971) pointed out, "All you learn from failing is how to fail." A student cannot learn adequately unless he is performing well. We accept and expect a range of grades, so we accept and expect a range of performance levels. We should not be accepting of this. High levels of performance need to be made possible for all students.

Good performance means more than simply getting good grades. It means that the daily work being done by the students is being done correctly and successfully. More simply put, you must get the right answers in order to learn the right answers. Much more will be said about the issue of success and failure in the next two chapters. For now, it should be noted that success is fundamental to achievement. Lack of success means lack of achievement. Failing grades are indicative of our failure to provide success for most students who receive them.

Low achieving and disadvantaged students should not be penalized simply because they are low achievers. They deserve work that they can do successfully. They deserve it not only for humane reasons but because success is necessary for adequate achievement. Lack of success produces the myriad of problems the low achieving and disadvantaged students have.

The requirement that all students must be successful is contradictory to a grading system. If all students must be successful, then it will be demonstrated in the work they do. They will be showing the same performance or scores on the work they are doing as their high achieving peers. Granted, the work will be at different levels of difficulty, but the indexes of performance (the scores) will be the same. Since the scores must be uniformly high, it will be virtually impossible to have a grading system of the type we do now.

Grades are not passive indexes of student performance. They are not just a symptom of low achievement. The existence of grades is a definite, active contributory factor in the educational difficulties of low achieving and disadvantaged students.

Chapter 8

FAILURE

Failure is the constant companion of low achieving and disadvantaged students in most of their school experience. Failure is unfortunately the antithesis of achievement. Students must do well to learn. They must get the correct answers regularly in order to learn the correct answers. The lack of achievement in these students is directly attributable to their chronic failure.

Failure has other terribly negative consequences in addition to preventing achievement. Permitting or requiring failure should be eliminated as an educational practice with low achieving and disadvantaged students. It is the principle cause of their problems.

Constant failure teaches a student to give up when encountering any instructional task (Grimes, 1981). Learned helplessness is one quite negative consequence of failing whenever a student attempts to understand or engage in an instructional activity.

Failure is damaging to a student's self-esteem. A student needs a reasonable level of success in order to develop a sense of confidence and competence. Failure is a direct attack on these, with consequent damage to a student's self-concept.

Adolescence is a difficult and emotional enough time for students already. Problems with self-esteem abound. Failure is not confidence-inspiring at any age, but it has even more profound consequences when it is imposed on the adolescent student. Failure in these instances is directly related to emotional and behavioral problems.

Chronic failure ultimately produces a discrepancy between a student's achievement and his aptitude for achievement. Failure is at best non-productive in regard to achievement. When students fail, their achievement is not progressing along with their potential to achieve. The longer failure occurs, the greater this discrepancy becomes.

Many states use a discrepancy formula for qualifying students as learning disabled. The thought behind this procedure is that if a child is achieving at or close to his potential for achievement, then his learning ability could not be considered impaired. What constitutes a significant discrepancy between aptitude and achievement varies considerably from one locale to another. However, the factor that does not vary in this system is that failure must occur for a sufficient length of time to impair achievement progress. The development of a significant discrepancy can take a long painful period of time. Unfortunately, it is the process through which low achieving students become classified as learning disabled. It is the process that has dramatically increased the numbers of learning disabled students in recent years. Failure has become the instrument used to produce handicapped students within our own educational system. Unfortunately, the instrument is wielded by the very agency that is supposed to be helping children.

The method of calculating the discrepancy varies, but measures of aptitude and achievement are similar. An individual test of intelligence is usually used as the measure of aptitude or potential for achievement. Standardized achievement tests are used as the measures of achievement. What constitutes a significant discrepancy between the two is the subject of some controversy, but the discrepancy must be substantial. For example, some might judge a difference of more than one year to be significant. A ten-year-old child with an IQ of ninety would have a mental age of nine. He would be expected to achieve at least as well as the average nine-year-old, or fourth grader. In order to achieve the year's discrepancy, this student's achievement test must indicate performance no greater than the third grade.

Some discrepancy formulas use arithmetic calculations based on statistical characteristics of the tests. The simpler ones only require that there be at least a difference of one standard deviation between achievement and aptitude. Some of the others are more complex and conservative. They can require even greater discrepancies before they are judged significant.

Discrepancy definitions of learning disabilities seem to legitimize failure. They certainly require failure for an extended period of time in order that the discrepancy emerge. Consider the ten-year-old mentioned earlier. In order for him to develop a one-year discrepancy between his achievement and potential for achievement, it will require him to fail for at least two years. When he enters the first grade he will have a mental age of 5.4. He will have a mental age of 6.3 at the beginning of second grade. Very little progress could be expected, and the child is likely to demonstrate very little. At the beginning of the third grade the child will have a mental age of 7.2. It is only by about this time that a child could be considered to have the one-year discrepancy, that is, if he has made no achievement progress. He has the potential to read as well as a beginning second grader, but he is still performing like a child starting first grade. Here, we have the year's difference necessary, but we have permitted the child to make no progress for at least two years in order to qualify for help.

A more likely scenario is that the child will make marginal progress. Failure may not be complete and abject but will be experienced in sufficient amounts to retard achievement but not stall it altogether. The length of time required for this low achieving student to develop a significant discrepancy may be considerably greater. However, this could not be considered a heartening prospect.

It is unfortunate that children are required to fail and achieve less than their potential in order to receive help. This just should not be our practice. Still, these students may be more fortunate than those low achieving students who somehow manage to achieve close to their potential but still experience failure because they are graded based on norms of their classmates rather than their own aptitude.

I have too seldom found low achieving students who have survived high school, let alone making achievement progress that matches their capacity. On those rare occasions that I have found low achieving students surviving in regular high school classrooms, with what is for them adequate achievement, their existence was not pleasant. For example, take the boy with the IQ of ninety mentioned earlier. Suppose that instead of falling behind his potential he has somehow continued to achieve as well as he could. When he is fifteen and about a tenth grader, if he is achieving to his capacity, he would be performing about like the average eighth grader. Even though he has made excellent achievement progress, he will still have trouble dealing with tenth grade level work if he is required to perform in a typical academic curriculum. He will likely be failing in several of the more academic classes.

This student, still faced with failure, does not have bright prospects if he is held to regular academic standards. He may be under pressure to drop out. His prospects for graduation may be dim. He is not experiencing much success in his required classes, and he feels helpless about doing anything to improve his lot.

It is interesting to note that I have never found a low achieving, disadvantaged student who had managed to achieve up to capacity. The double problem (disadvantage and low achievement) has been too difficult to overcome. Those low achieving students who manage adequate achievement usually do so because of helpful intervention from outside the school. Those children with capable, concerned family will receive much supplementary help, maybe in the form of assistance with homework or through tutoring. Their achievement will be in large part due to parental assistance. Disadvantaged students are unlikely to have families that can be such resources.

Low achieving students unfortunately experience failure even if they are achieving up to their potential. This is because rigid curriculum structure demands grade level performance. Achievement to potential should be an honored objective for low achieving students. It is too bad that even in achieving it they still may be casualties of unforgiving curricula.

There are specific reasons for failure. I have mentioned the reasons in very general terms so far. Fundamentally, failure results from the difficulty a task has for a given student. But what makes a task too difficult? Basically, a task is too difficult if it has too many unknown parts, too many parts requiring skills as yet unattained by the individual trying to perform it. There may be too many unknown words in a reading selection for a student to both identify those words and comprehend the meaning. In an arithmetic activity, the problem may require the use of a variety of subskills that a student has not yet mastered. An assignment may introduce more new items than a particular student can manage to cope with given his short-term memory limitations.

Failure can be described by arbitrary cutoff scores, or subjective standards. It is a subjective issue where an "F" should be assigned on the grading scale. Should it be given at 69, 65, 64, or 59 percent accuracy? Is credit given for getting parts of a problem right without getting its correct answer? Probably no standards are more varied and unreliable than those used to judge written composition. Here, the standards are the most arbitrarily used in any of the subject areas.

The most objective methods of determining failure from a student's perspective have come from the literature associated with curriculum-based assessment (Hargis, 1987).

The difficulty of a task becomes too great when it affects a student's ability to remain engaged in doing it. This engagement in instructional activities is called academically engaged time or academic learning time. The amount of time so spent is directly related to achievement. If a task is too difficult, the student will not be able to effectively engage in it, and so academically engaged time is reduced or eliminated.

When does a task become so difficult that a student falls off-task and cannot remain reasonably engaged in learning. Emmett Betts (1946) first described this point in reading difficulty. He said that when a student encounters more than about 4 percent unknown words in a reading selection, his comprehension of the passage will drop and he will show the signs of off-task behavior. If a student cannot comprehend a passage, he is not really engaged in reading it. If he cannot comprehend it, he will probably begin to show signs of frustration and agitation. Betts called this boundary the frustration level. It is the point where failure could be said to begin in reading.

In drill and seat work activities, there is also a point also where students begin to go off-task and show signs of frustration. The boundaries are not as precise as a single figure would suggest, so a range of 20 to 30 percent is used. For example, in drill activity on some subtraction facts done on a worksheet, if a student is unable to do more than 30 percent of the items, he will begin to show signs of frustration and off-task behavior.

Basically, failure, from a student's perspective, occurs when the difficulty of the task becomes sufficiently great that his engagement in it is curtailed and he is no longer learning. It is not true that things are not learned when task difficulty becomes too great. A student is always in danger of learning the wrong answer, and he is certainly learning to dislike and to avoid these frustrating tasks. Learned helplessness is also an unfortunate outcome of frustration level activities.

A student faced with tasks that are too difficult may resort to purposeless random guessing. He may have insufficient known context in a reading passage to even make anything other than a random guess for each of the numerous unknown words he encounters. He is so overwhelmed by the number of unknowns that the use of decoding skills forces him to almost a standstill of painful word-by-word sounding out. Such behavior is labeled word-calling.

In math activities, especially the repetitive, drill activities, there is a great risk of learning wrong answers. In drill activities, a student has the opportunity to repeat wrong answers. In effect, he may be getting drill, not on the correct answer, but on the wrong answer. It is in this way that error patterns are acquired. Error patterns can emerge through the practice of erroneous response strategies, some of which simply have started as random guesses. At any rate these are learned response patterns, and they cause more problems than not knowing an answer at all (Ashlock, 1986).

Drill activities should be made up largely of items that a student can do correctly but not yet quickly, easily, or automatically. Students should not have the opportunity to practice errors. Frustration and failure level work often provide more opportunity for practicing errors than for practicing correct responses.

Continued failure experiences may produce a variety of learned error patterns and negative or ineffective approaches to learning. For this reason, students that have experienced extended periods of failure require remedial instruction. Remedial instruction is time consuming and labor intensive. The problem behaviors the students have learned must be identified, unlearned and replaced by the appropriate response or strategy. Identifying the many different problems can be a difficult, occasionally mystifying problem. The reason for these problems is practice at the failure level. Failure should be avoided to prevent the need for remedial instruction.

Written composition activities pose especially difficult problems for low achieving students. It was mentioned earlier that standards of scoring or grading written composition are the most arbitrary and varied. When students attempt written expression, they are often overwhelmed by the many red marks and poor grades they receive. There will be so many places where the students make mistakes that they will not likely benefit from correction. There will be just too many different problems marked for them to focus on any one. The students may feel no hope for success in written composition and attempt to avoid the activity altogether. Success at written composition is frustratingly illusive because of the ambiguous and unreliable standards used to score and grade it, and because low achieving students will make many more mistakes than their higher achieving peers. In order to avoid the frustration they feel any time they produce written composition, they may limit and restrict their output so that there will be less material to receive criticism for. Failure for these students means less and less practice on a skill that requires a great deal of practice.

Because of working at frustration and failure levels, low achieving students miss the important practice necessary to achieve mastery and fluency in math, reading and writing activities. Skills, if acquired at all, seem to be held in the most tenuous, uncertain way.

Practice, in a conventional sense, is seldom possible for the low achiever. Practice should be done with facts and skills that are learned but have not acquired the degree of mastery that make them fluent and automatic. Practice is needed for the transition of words, facts, and skills from short- to long-term memory. Low achieving students cannot make the transition to long-term memory, because it was not learned well enough to lodge in short-term memory in the first place. Too many newly introduced unknowns are accumulating with the previously introduced, but still unlearned, unknowns. These are overwhelming demands placed on the memory capacity as well as the learning capacity of these students.

Practice or repetition is only effective if, at each repetition, the student gets it right. If he gets it wrong, he learns nothing, or, worse, he learns it wrong.

The more you engage effectively in an activity, the better you get at it. This is true until you reach the limits of your talent. This is as true of learning to read as it is of learning to play golf, to play a musical instrument, or to be a mechanic. The opposite is also true. If you engage in an activity ineffectively or poorly, you will probably not improve and may even get worse. These phenomena produce what are called Matthew effects (Stanovich, 1986; Hargis et al., 1988). Matthew effects are "the-rich-get-richer-and-the-poor-get-poorer" phenomenon.

As a student acquires reading skill, opportunities for reading open all around him. Print is everywhere. Reading is used in all subject areas. A rich reading environment opens itself to the student who succeeds. Countless opportunities for practice occur. It appears that reading progress occurs in the most able students in an explosion that far exceeds the rate at which instruction is proceeding. It is as if the students were teaching themselves; in a way they are.

On the other hand, the student who fails, not only appears to make no progress, he seems to do worse as time goes on. He cannot benefit from all the incidental opportunities for reading practice that surround him. He is not able to use reading in other subject areas. He cannot read for fun. He falls farther and farther behind his higher achieving peers and farther and farther behind his own potential. He feels increasingly frustrated, helpless, and ineffective. This still further compounds the problem.

Failure is unfortunately an institutionalized part of our system. We expect failure because it is part of our grading system. Failure is our primary diagnostic tool. A student must fail and do so substantially before anything is done. Often, what is done is only an attempt to fit the student into the system. Efforts are not directly addressed to the problem, which is failure. The most common intervention is simply to repeat grades. This is done in the old lock-step without regard to the student's specific instructional level where he might hope to work without failure and frustration.

There are a number of reasons that failure occurs. These reasons have been addressed in this section of the book. However, for low achieving students, it is their primary educational experience. Success is the principle need of low achieving and disadvantaged students. The remainder of the book is devoted to the changes and remedies needed so that these students can experience success and achievement.

Chapter 9

SUCCESS

An overlooked and undervalued principle of learning is that
success is the primary ingredient of achievement. Success is the
principle ingredient in learning. If one gets the right answer, then one
learns the right answer. The conditions for getting the right answers
must be set up for low achieving and disadvantaged students. These
conditions are currently missing from their experience.

Matthew effects were mentioned in the previous chapter. The "poor-
get-poorer" effects were discussed in regard to the failure experiences
that plague low achieving and disadvantaged students. Success character-
izes the "rich-get-richer" side of the Matthew effects. These are the effects
that optimize success in achievement.

The concept of Matthew effects comes from the Gospel according to
Saint Matthew.

> For whosoever hath, to him shall be given, and he shall have more
> abundance: but whosoever hath not, from him shall be taken away even
> that he hath." (XIII:12)
> For unto everyone that hath shall be given, and he shall have
> abundance: but from him that hath not shall be taken away even that
> which he hath. (XXV:29)

Stanovich (1986) described Matthew effects in regard to learning to
read. He states that the very children who are reading well and who have
good vocabularies will read more, learn more word meanings through
reading and thereby learn to read even better. Matthew effects have been
shown to be an important source of the variation in achievement in
many curricular areas. They need to be considered, particularly in
regard to low achieving and disadvantaged students.

Matthew effects can be compounding when students are failing. Failure compounds the Matthew effect. It accounts for underachievement
and the emergence of the discrepancy between achievement and potential.
Remember, however, that success alone does not cure individual dif-

ferences. Differences in achievement are naturally wide and widen more as students move through school.

Success is needed to keep the students' achievement at an individually optimal level. It should eliminate most underachievement. If low achieving students experience success and enter the "rich-get-richer" cycle, maybe their achievement level can exceed our current expectations for their performance; and since Matthew effects in reading are mutually enhancing with other cognitive skill areas, a child's potential for achievement may actually increase. This is certainly more likely to be the case for disadvantaged students.

We in education should be duty bound to make certain that all children both have and be given success in the abundance mentioned in the Gospel according to Matthew. Success for most low achieving and disadvantaged students must be given; it must be structured into their curriculum. Success for these children is not something they can will themselves to do consciously. In current curricular structures these children neither have nor receive success. They are forced into the "poor-get-poorer" cycle by our lock-step system. We make them curriculum casualties.

So, success is fundamentally important to achievement; let's insure it. But what is it we should do? What specifically is success? How do we make a student succeed? Do we hand out trophies and ribbons? Do we simply put stars, smiley faces, or A's on papers? Some of the answers to these questions are determined by how we define success.

The definition of success and the procedures for making sure a student experiences it are fairly simple and straightforward. This is true even though they are not widely known.

We must take our definition from observations of students we know are achieving and succeeding well. Success means that you are able to accomplish a task. The task is completed and it or its constituents are done correctly. In learning, tasks must be done correctly. You only learn something if you get it right a sufficient number of times to commit it to long-term memory storage. The first component of success-based instruction is that a student must be given tasks that can be done correctly. This may mean breaking some tasks into smaller, more manageable substeps that can be performed with success before tackling the larger, more complex one.

In reading, a new word must be identified correctly a sufficient number of times to make it familiar and instantly recognizable. In math, the correct answer for each multiplication fact must be identified correctly a sufficient number of times so the answer comes automatically. The sequence of procedures that make up long division must be conducted correctly with sufficient repetition so that the correct procedures are performed automatically when long division is called for.

Repetition is fundamental to learning. Repetition has two functions. First, it is used to maintain information temporarily in short-term memory, and second to create memory traces with some permanence in long-term memory. In short, you need practice to learn almost anything. Some people learn very quickly. The amount of repetition they need may be relatively small. If the task they are learning is in an area of their talent or aptitude, the learning is quick and easy. At the other end of the learning continuum are the people who require a great deal of repetition to learn. Need for repetition is an individual matter and is on a wide distribution in any classroom.

The success element in repetition is too often overlooked. Teachers will say something like, "He's been over it a thousand times and he still can't do it"; or "He's gone over it again and again, but he only gets it right half the time." What is overlooked in these problem situations is the success element. Each repetition is only an effective repetition if a student gets the practice item correct. If a student gets the same wrong answer each time, he is likely to learn it wrong; it will be a learned error or error pattern. If the student gets it right only part of the time, the effect will be to show inconsistency in response to it later. If the student makes no attempt to respond at each repetition, the repetition counts for nothing except lost time.

Remember, a repetition is only a real repetition if the students get it right. The unfamiliar printed word is associated with the familiar spoken word, either by decoding or by telling. Each arithmetic fact must get the correct answer associated with each pair of numbers. The number of times the practice item is presented in text, worksheet, or flash card does not count. It is only the number of correct answers to each repetition that counts. The number of wrong, uncorrected answers will actually detract from the learning process. A student must succeed and show evidence of success at each step in drill and practice.

If the students gets everything right, what is the challenge? The answer to this question requires a distinction be made between work and busy-work. In the routine of schoolwork, new items from the curriculum are being introduced. As mentioned earlier, these new items may need practice to process them from short-term to more permanent memory storage. This is work and it must be done successfully. On the other hand, busy-work is simply giving students work that already is in the stage of permanent storage; it is already mastered and automatic. Work like this is given simply to occupy time. It is useless activity.

Doing good work, even though the accuracy and scores indicate success, is challenging. However, the challenge should never exceed a student's ability to demonstrate this high performance level.

Low achieving students are challenged far too much. They should be challenged at the same level as their higher achieving peers. The work may be proceeding at a different tempo, but the maximum benefits to the students only occur when performance is very high. The performance scores should be in the same bands for both low and high achieving students, even though the amount of curricular ground covered will be different.

When the performance scores are the same for both groups, Matthew effects will benefit the low achievers as well. Granted, there will be differences in benefits, but benefits there will be. The person with five gold talents will still end up with ten, but now the person who started with one will end with two rather than none.

As Forell (1985) pointed out, we have a double standard in regard to challenge: high success, comfortable difficulty for high achievers; little success, frustrating difficulty for low achievers. This double standard must be eliminated.

What is this level of difficulty? How can it be measured? It must advance the student on the curricular path. It is directly measurable in important instructional activities. The specifics of incorporating the success level in instructional activity will be covered in subsequent chapters. For the moment, a brief description will do. Emmett Betts (1946) defined difficulty levels in regard to reading. In general terms he said that reading material is of an appropriate difficulty level for instructional purposes if a student encounters new words in the range of 2 to 4 percent and can comprehend 75 percent of the questions directed at its content. Material that exceeds 4 percent unfamiliar words and/or produces lower comprehension is entering the frustration level of difficulty.

Betts cited another important success level reading activity. He called it the basal or independent level of difficulty. Here, a student would encounter fewer than 2 percent unfamiliar words and would comprehend at least 90 percent of questions directed to the selection. A student would need no instructional assistance or introduction to read this material.

He could manage it independently; hence its name. This level would be suitable for recreational reading. This level is important for developing mastery and fluency in reading. It is also important in helping students learn to enjoy reading and encouraging them to read more. This is definitely an important constituent of the Matthew effect.

For drill and seatwork activities, there are somewhat different guidelines (Gickling and Thompson, 1985). The higher the performance level, the better. Remember, it is not profitable to practice errors. Ninety to 100 percent accuracy is desirable for these activities. However, an accuracy level of 70 to 80 percent will be sufficiently comfortable for most students to keep them engaged and feeling successful. This level does permit much opportunity for error practice and can be used only when immediate feedback can be provided and the errors corrected forthwith.

For individual students the number of newly introduced items will be quite variable on drill and seatwork activities, though the overall scores should be in the same range. Some students can concentrate on a few new items, while others can be drilled on many more simultaneously. Miller's (1956) magic number, seven plus or minus two, suggests a rough range for an introduction rate. Low achieving students will be at the low end of the range. Ultimately, the number of new items that can be introduced can only be determined by checking a student's performance on activities where the number of new items is varied. The overall scores must indicate success. More will be said on the specifics of this in later chapters.

Of all the things that might be done for or given to a student to motivate him to learn, success is the most important. Skinner (1972) pointed out the power of success as a reinforcer. The next most reinforcing thing a student receives is accomplishment. Tasks are completed. Of course task completion is actually a constituent of success. In order to be successful, one must complete the task. I should add that this is enormously reinforcing to teachers as well. There is nothing quite so important to teachers as having students completing their work and doing well at it.

A necessary condition for success and task completion is academically engaged time (Rosenshine and Berliner, 1978) or academic learning time (Gickling and Thompson, 1985). Achievement is directly proportional to the amount of time engaged in a learning activity. The necessary condition for engaged time is success. Appropriate difficulty of a task permits success and permits and reinforces a student's attention and engagement in it. Success produces achievement through engagement with learning activities. All these are reciprocally reinforcing.

The more time a student spends engaged in learning, the less time he spends off-task. Off-task time is a product of task difficulty. A student can't remain indefinitely engaged in a task that is too difficult. A student can't really be engaged in something that is too difficult to do. He will be doing nothing more than staring at the work or, possibly worse, doing it wrong. Time off-task engages a teacher's time more than time engaged in learning. Students will be doing something else if they are not working. This activity may be passive daydreaming in some students, but it may be disruptive overt activity in others. A teacher's time is consumed by off-task behavior. Time is better spent preparing engaging, success-producing activities that keep time off-task to a minimum.

Students can only learn good work habits and have good attitudes toward work if they are given work that they can do and learn to do better. Work that does not permit a student to be engaged in it only teaches a student poor work habits and produces negative attitudes toward work. A student that continually fails is repelled by learning activities and learns to avoid them.

Success and achievement are important for maintaining an adequate self-concept in students in regard to school. Certainly, failure is damaging and should be avoided. Educational institutions that require success in students will be held in far greater esteem as well. Low achieving and disadvantaged students currently regard our educational systems with apprehension, fear, distrust, or dislike. Institutions that impose failure on students cannot be viewed positively by them. Low achieving students cannot feel that our educational institutions care for or respect them. This only fosters negative feelings on the part of these students toward our educational system.

Low achieving students make up the bulk of high school dropouts. They are really forced out by the failure imposed on them. These students need not be forced out. Institutionalizing success as a condition of instructional delivery is necessary. The institution that is supposed to provide free public education to all students should do just that. This will require a change in the way we view low achieving students.

Requiring success for each student will demand different procedures for the identification and teaching of learning disabled and behavior-disordered students. If low achieving students are experiencing success, their achievement will match their aptitude, no achievement/IQ discrepancy will emerge as it now does in so many low achieving students. The dropout rate will decline markedly, and the number of students with learning disabilities and behavior disorders will decline dramatically. Failure cannot be our primary diagnostic tool if success is required.

Only the students who are still having learning problems and demonstrating problem behavior will likely be "real" learning disabled students. Their numbers will be many fewer than are currently so labeled. Behavior and difficulty that persists in the face of planned success is likely to be a problem originating in the student rather than the curriculum. In these cases, students demonstrating learning and behavior problems should receive special help.

We mislead ourselves by assuming that learning problems are in the student rather than the curriculum. We make ourselves look ineffective by ignoring the important role that success plays in handling low achieving students. Time and time again the following events take place because of this error: Students are judged behavior-disordered when their behavior becomes so disruptive that they can't be managed in the regular classroom. They are then placed in a special classroom. The special teacher will have students who are achieving at a variety of levels and will receive new students routinely at any time during the year. The special teacher is prepared to place the student at whatever instructional level the student can work on. The pressures of failure are immediately removed, and the student's behavior almost immediately changes. Observers of these classrooms remark that the behavior of these students seems no different than any other students. Why most of these students are in these classrooms is a question frequently raised. Change the environment from one of failure to one of success and the behavior changes.

Unfortunately, the change in behavior is assumed to be the result of a change in the student, not simply a change resulting from the new environment. The student is believed cured after awhile and is returned to the regular classroom. The student experiences failure and frustration again. The old behavior patterns re-emerge and the student goes back to special education or drops out.

We view success as something that must be achieved only through strenuous competition. This is a grand mistake. We must plan success for all students.

Chapter 10

TESTS AND THE CURRICULUM

Much testing that goes on in schools has little direct relationship to instructional activity. Tests are used to give grades and to qualify students for special placement. Both of these uses are for the most part fundamentally inappropriate. But what are appropriate uses for tests, particularly in regard to low achieving and disadvantaged students?

Two overridingly important functions of tests are: to help prevent a student from failing and to insure a student's success. These are not just two different ways of saying the same thing, though they are obviously related.

The first place in which failure should be prevented is before it has a chance to occur. Usually, the first opportunity to use tests to head off failure is in kindergarten. Here, readiness tests are are usually norm-referenced tests that reflect the range of readiness for academic instruction that exists in the standardization group. Children who demonstrate lack of readiness for beginning academic instruction on these tests are very likely to have problems and experience failure in school. Also, kindergarten teachers' informal assessment is likely to be accurate in identifying which of their children are not mature enough to succeed in first grade. Information from informal assessment like this, as well as the formal assessment provided in the readiness tests, can indicate which children are likely to experience failure. This information should be acted upon. There is no reason to send immature children on to stressful failure experiences. We have the misguided notions that it is worse to hold them back in kindergarten and that they must keep up with their age peers.

Placing students at any point on the curriculum should be done with the view of finding a level where the students won't fail. When students transfer to a different school system, or when they need to begin studying different subject areas, are the times that assessment information should

69

be used to protect them from failure. Tests made of the scope and sequence of skills on the school's curriculum (curriculum-referenced tests) and achievement test information can be used to judge if the student is sufficiently able to move into the new study area or at what level the student has entry or readiness skills. All placement decisions should be based on finding a position on the curriculum where the student is likely to succeed. If placement decisions are made based on chronological age or current grade placement without regard to actual achievement level, students are at risk for failure.

Avoiding failure is important. Insuring that students are continuing to be successful is another important dimension of testing. Testing for success in instruction is the ongoing form of assessment that must be incorporated in all instructional activity.

Matching the curriculum level with the students' entry level skills is necessary to avoid failure and optimize the likelihood of success, but maintaining the match on a day-to-day basis is necessary to actually produce success and achievement.

The next purpose of assessment is to track and report progress. Much assessment is simply used to give grades. The expression "evaluate progress" means assign a rating or grade. In the majority of cases, it will be a letter grade or comparable number rating, or it may simply be the alternative, pass/fail or satisfactory/no progress.

Progress cannot be adequately reported by grades. They give absolutely no specific information about where the student is on the curricular sequence, how much progress he has made over any time frame, or what objectives set for him have been attained. Altogether too much (any would be too much in my opinion) assessment effort is devoted to giving grades. This effort should be devoted to the important purposes of assessment, namely, avoiding failure, insuring success, and truly measuring progress.

The measurement of progress lends itself to another important reason for assessment. This is accountability. By accountability, I mean the evaluation of the educational delivery system itself. The evaluation of the quality of teaching, the effectiveness of instructional methods and materials, or the effect of the environment or educational placement. We need to evaluate what we do in the education of these students.

Teaching, or, more precisely, the effect of teaching, can be evaluated several ways. All of them require evaluation of student performance. Student progress should be measured relative to themselves. This requires plotting change in performance over time. This measurement should be done with both norm-referenced and curriculum-referenced tests. Periodic measurements should be taken to evaluate progress over standard periods of time. Norm-referenced tests are commonly administered annually already. Usually, they are administered at the end of each school year. If the norm-referenced tests have reasonable content validity, they may be used to check students' progress over time. The effectiveness of what happened during that time period can then be subject to evaluation given this information.

Curriculum-referenced tests should be used to gain more specific information. Tests that measure progress along the specific curriculum being used will be given over standard time periods. These tests give more precise indication of what curricular objectives have been attained. These tests measure the effectiveness of instruction in regard to specific curricular objectives. They also give specific information about a student's current level of readiness and what instructional materials and activities may likely be used with success with him.

Both test types—norm-referenced and curriculum-referenced tests—are useful in the measurement of instructional effectiveness. This measurement can be done fairly if consideration is given to where the students started at the beginning of the evaluation period, and how similar students might be expected to perform.

Teachers with low achieving and disadvantaged students may be fearful of the evaluation of instruction because achievement progress in their students, even at best, is not as rapid as in more able students. Consideration must be given to these teachers by gauging progress given where their students started and how they do relative to other similar students in the general population. A combination of norm-referenced and curriculum-referenced tests are needed to fairly judge the quality of instruction with these students.

A student's progress along the curriculum should be continually evaluated given curriculum-referenced tests. The curriculum itself should be considered a test. The scope and sequence of skills that comprise the curriculum should be an inventory for measuring student performance. This insures the content validity of the measuring device. Testing what you are teaching is insured. A student's placement on the curricular sequence can be judged accurately.

If the curriculum has the form of an inventory or test, it may encourage more individual treatment of students. It will if the student is permitted to work at the level on the curriculum where he actually can perform adequately. All curricula should be assigned to students, not to grade levels. Students should be permitted to work along the curricular path from their personal starting point and proceed at the rate at which they experience success. A curriculum inventory should be an individual map given to each student to keep him moving successfully along the curricular route.

The starting point on the curricular map is very important to students. Finding the right place is how failure is avoided in the first place. Avoiding failure, as was pointed out earlier, is a primary function of testing. Unless preschool and kindergarten become still more academic, the usual starting place for academic instruction is the first grade. Before students begin first grade, they are typically given readiness tests to see if they have sufficient maturity to begin. These tests are not usually curriculum-referenced tests. They are norm-referenced tests that must have reasonable predictive validity in order to be useful. In particular, these tests should predict which students will fail. The students who perform in the failure range on readiness tests should not enter first grade. They should remain in kindergarten until they clearly demonstrate the ability to proceed successfully in first grade.

Norm-referenced readiness tests have one main shortcoming. They do not measure all of the things that may contribute to student failure. A student's health, vision, hearing, and family condition may also influence his academic performance. Teacher observation and informal inquiry should supplement readiness tests to make certain that children who are at risk for failure are protected.

At any transition point during the school years the readiness of the students needs evaluation. This is not readiness of the sort just mentioned. It is the entry level skill, the preparedness level of the student. Does a student have the prerequisite skills for taking the geometry class? Does the nine-year-old transferring to a new school have the reading and arithmetic background to be placed in the fourth grade?

Entry level skills are most accurately assessed using inventories drawn from the curriculum itself. The skills mastered can be identified and the entry level of the student can be compared to the requirements of the course or grade level.

There should be a far more structured connection between tests and curricula. Curricula should be written in the form of inventories or checklists so that a student's progress along it can be measured. Entry or readiness levels of students would be more apparent.

This relationship between curriculum and measurement insures validity of the measurement being done. The measurement is useful; it is obviously related to instruction. It makes teaching the test a practical necessity, not a pejorative expression.

The taxonomy of curricular items, the scope and sequence of skills contained on the curriculum should be used to construct inventories. These inventories should be used to determine placement of students in transition and to track progress.

Testing in this manner would be done to make a match between instructional level and student. Progress would be reportable directly and specifically in terms of accomplishments and achievement on the curriculum. Testing should be done for making the match, not for giving grades.

Curriculum-based testing (which this is) would discourage the practice of giving tests to determine grades. Curricula could be assigned to students rather than to grades. Students would work at a level on the curriculum where they could achieve best. They would not be compelled to fit the lock-step grades where components of the curriculum are currently assigned.

Testing for grades discourages assigning the curriculum to individuals. When we need to assign grades, there is a need for a degree of mismatch. A certain number of students are needed who are not up to the skill level of the curriculum in each grade. They will be the ones receiving the poor grades. We need them to prevent grade inflation. We need poor grades to show that we have high standards.

It is ironic that we have need to make students get poor grades, and when they do we wonder why. As a consequence we give special tests (which are not curriculum-based) to find the reason for the poor grades. These diagnostic tests measure a range of theoretical constructs that range over such things as psycholinguistic ability, learning style, auditory or visual perception, brain waves, etc. Inevitably, weakness will be found, and if this information is acted upon, the student will be launched into a new curriculum prescribed to ameliorate the assumed weakness. The students seldom ever benefit from such approaches. They are very likely to improve their performance on the special curriculum. However, since this area of work had nothing to do with the students' failure in the first place, no improvement in academic performance will be noted. In fact, students will likely be worse off. Time they might otherwise have spent working in the regular curriculum has been diverted to the special curriculum. Students may actually regress as a result of such programs.

If we want improved performance on the curriculum, then we should work specifically on the curriculum. Our testing, therefore, should be curriculum-based. This insures that we stay on track and helps us recognize that a student's failure is, for the most part, the result of a mismatch between what we are teaching and what he is actually capable of learning.

Be very careful how you choose your tests. Consider first their content validity. Are they comprised of what is being taught? Better still, construct test items from each item on the curriculum, then validity is not a problem.

Many special education teachers who are not so constrained by giving grades and meeting grade level curricular demands, prepare curricula that are based on tests. Comprehensive tests, the types which are often marketed as being criterion-referenced, frequently test a broad scope-and-sequence of skills in various curricular areas. Since they cover a curricular area, it makes sense to teach to the areas covered on the test. If the test covers skills deemed important, then it is sensible to teach those skills. The tests, then, form the curriculum being taught. Certainly, if the test outlines the significant areas of study for particular students, this is a perfectly logical approach.

Minimum competency tests or proficiency tests have come into increasingly frequent use. These tests supposedly measure the skills that are the minimum acceptable for students who are to graduate from high school. These tests now have gained great importance, because they have become the requirement for graduation or the barrier preventing graduation. Since it is so important that these tests be passed, their content has become the focus of curriculum development.

This is eminently logical. If the tests measure important things, then those things should be taught. This relationship between minimum competency tests and curriculum offers real, positive opportunities for low achieving and disadvantaged students. The objectives and standards set by the tests are typically within the threshold of the potential for achievement that these students have.

Critics of minimum competency testing suggest that it lowers the standards for all students. Actually, they provide standards at an attainable level for low achieving and even most mildly handicapped students. We should not hold all students to standards determined by average performance. This is true for high achieving students as well. Students should be assisted in moving through the curriculum at whatever rate and to the highest end their talent permits.

Minimum competency tests simply establish a minimum level on the curriculum at which a student should achieve and still be considered qualified for a high school diploma. If the objectives listed on a minimum competency test vary from those on the regular curriculum, then the differences should be minimized to close the validity gap between test and curriculum. Tests should be intimately related to instruction. Teaching to tests should be standard practice as long as the tests measure important curricular items. This should almost always be the case.

Routine instructional activity should have measurement embedded in it. One might say the activity must be evaluated in regard to a student's performance while engaged in it. The reverse is usually the case. The student's performance on doing the activity is graded.

Since a student's performance must be very good to indicate successful engagement in an activity, the scores on it must reflect this fact. If the scores fall off, the activity must be altered so the student can retain maximum benefits from it. Routine evaluation must change its focus. The purpose of routine testing should be for maintaining the match between instructional activity and student ability level. Testing for grades contradicts this important purpose.

Progress can be tracked more specifically and meaningfully by using curriculum-based tests that report where a student is and what the student is doing on his curriculum. Norm-referenced tests can be used if relative performance information is desired. The norms give a basis for comparing students to various standard groups.

Chapter 11

TESTS AS INSTRUCTION

Instructional activity itself should be used as the primary means of testing. This is not testing in the formal sense we usually think of. It is an informal procedure. The reason for the importance of using instructional activity as a form of testing is that it is the only way we can evaluate a student's performance while engaged in learning. It is the most direct form of assessment. We are not making guesses about placing students in the right position on the curriculum. We are directly observing performance at that place. We then can make accurate judgments about the adequacy of that placement. Quite practically, the proof of the pudding is in the eating. The proof of the placement is a student's performance in classroom work after the placement has been made. After initial placement, specific adjustments in the curricular activity given a student can be made only after evaluating his work while doing it.

Initial placements should be made by means of curricular inventories, inventories which are made up of sampled items from the curriculum. Placement should be made by checking the mastery level on the inventory. The correct items suggest the skills the student has learned and show the threshold or entry position on the curriculum.

Adequacy of the placement made with this information can only be judged by observing and evaluating a student's performance once the placement has been made.

How is instruction to be used as a test? Actually, most instructional activity is already tested or used as a test. It is simply scored so a grade can be given and recorded. Any assignment, homework or seatwork can be and usually is scored or graded. The effects of instructional activity is already tested by periodic quizzes and tests. The same scoring practices can be used but with an entirely different purpose than giving a student a grade.

The activity itself should be graded in regard to its appropriateness for use with individual students. The scores should be used to tune or match the difficulty of the activity to the individual student. For example, if a student is given a quiz over something that was just introduced to check how much he had retained, a poor score would indicate that the presentation of the material was too difficult. It was too complex or contained more information than the student could assimilate. The presentation will have to be altered. It should present less or otherwise be reduced in difficulty so the student can retain it.

At the next level—the drill or practice level—the student is engaged alone in the activity. This could be homework or seatwork. Worksheet, board work, workbook activities, etc., are examples. This includes any activity where the student is engaged actively, not passively listening or watching. The student is practicing, trying to commit the knowledge to long-term memory, trying to increase his fluency in the skill.

At either level the student should be given no more information than he can manage. Some students can retain more information in short-term memory and practice on more at one time. Some students can cope with problems and directions with more steps and complexity than others. The only way one can find out how much a student can manage effectively is by assessing his performance while working with various introduction rates. A student should not be given a heavier burden than he can carry successfully.

Evidence of success is measured by the accuracy or correctness of the students' performance on any task. Students should be given no more new items or no more complex a task than they can do correctly in tests, drill, or seatwork. Ninety percent accuracy or better is desired. If the students can't get that level of accuracy, then the tasks must be adjusted so they can. Too many errors means too much opportunity to practice errors. Too many errors means a reduction in a student's rate of achievement.

The level should not be considered too easy. Remember, the highest achieving students, the ones with the best grades, perform at this level. It should be remembered, though, that the burden of complexity and rate of instruction should be the maximum that a student can handle and still get it done correctly. Remember, you only learn something if you get it correct enough times in practice activities so that it is retained with permanence in the correct form.

Instructional activity must always be viewed as assessment which needs scores in the 90 percent plus range. Instead of one level of instructional activity which produces variable scores in a classroom, the activities are made variable in difficulty to produce the same high scores in all students.

Everything a student does should be considered a test, but it should be considered a test of the activity with a view to changing it if it gets too low a score from a student.

The current practice of scoring papers and dutifully recording grades is a mindless practice and a waste of the most important assessment opportunity that occurs in school-instructional activity itself. Teachers should note the errors a student makes. This note should not be made in a grade book, but it should be noted for immediate correction. A student needs immediate feedback and correction. All too often students' papers are scored without attention to errors. Students should not be permitted to make an error and then repeat it. It is too often the case that the same mistake is made repeatedly on a paper and then made repeatedly on subsequent activities.

Errors are often no more to a teacher than a red mark to be recorded. The practice of scoring for grades needs to be changed. All instruction should be scored with a view to changing it to produce success and to catch and correct any mistakes.

Observing students while they are engaged in instructional activities is, and should be, used as the most frequent and direct form of assessment. While a student is doing the work is the best time to assess performance on it. Scoring work after it is produced is not nearly as useful. The best time to catch an error is when it occurs. Feedback is most prompt. The teacher will easily find the reason for the errors. There will be far less opportunity for practicing errors.

The most important aspect of teaching or instruction occurs when the student is engaged in the activity. The importance of academically engaged time to achievement has already been stressed. Learning is accomplished by doing. More time for doing must be provided during the school day. The time that is spent doing or engaged is also the best time to assess a student's performance. The question often arises as to how a teacher could have enough time to observe all the students. There are some techniques that permit the teacher to do more observing.

Classroom organizations that are student centered rather than teacher centered permit teachers to spend more time observing. Supervised study activities, peer tutoring, and cooperative learning arrangements are all designed to engage students in work during the school day. These arrangements, in fact, make the teachers' role more observational and supervisory.

One supervised study technique is like a step back in time. James Tucker told me that he feels there should be a chalkboard revival. He reminded me that a generation ago, three walls of the typical school room were covered by chalkboards. Board work was a routine of the day. After the teacher introduced something, the students practiced doing it at the chalkboard. The teacher could readily observe a large number of students. The effect of instruction could be directly observed and assessed, then adjustments made. Tucker feels that this wonderful medium for assessment fell from favor when the Ditto and Mimeograph machines became universally available. I agree with him. Reviving the use of chalkboards, of course, will not assure that they will be used for direct assessment. However, they physically provide a practical format for large numbers of students to engage in work that can be easily observed by a teacher.

Most work a student does should be evaluated in regard to matching the difficulty level of the work to the student as well as to catching errors and providing feedback. This is active assessment that assures success. It is informal, but it is systematic and constant to the point of being institutionalized.

How do you change from the practice of scoring to give grades to the practice of scoring to produce success? How do you do this with the routine activities of the day? Since good performance and success is the objective, use as the example the scores of the high achieving students in the room. These will be approximately the scores that you are seeking for each student. When performance on any activity falls below the example or standards set by the high achieving students, then the activity should be adjusted so that the good performance level is regained.

The same performance that is used to evaluate a student for grades, whether objective or subjective, should be used. The big difference is that emphasis on evaluation changes from the student to the instructional activity. Scores or performance information is used to evaluate an activity's difficulty in regard to the students' readiness for performing in it. The students must be performing well, so the activity may need to be adjusted in complexity or other activities from an earlier point on the curricular sequence selected.

The kinds of evaluative information already being collected does not have to change. The difference is that this information is not simply placed in a grade book. It is used to change or adjust the instructional activity. The adjustment or change is effective if it brings the students' performance up to the success level.

This informal assessment must be a part of all instructional activity. Watch to see if a student can stay engaged in an activity. Does he show signs of frustration? Is he off-task more than on? Did he do it correctly? What is he doing incorrectly? In sum, is each student doing well, and what is he doing incorrectly?

If he is not doing well, reduce the load to the point where he is doing well. If he is missing something, identify what he is doing wrong and give him the right answer or show him the correct way immediately. These activities are the fundamentals of assessment in instruction.

This kind of assessment is an active, integral part of instruction. It takes a new mind-set to use the same kind of evaluative information used to give grades to make changes in instructional activities. If this is really being done, the evaluative information will have absolutely no value in determining a grade distribution. There will no longer be a grade distribution! It is not possible to have both!

More instructional activity should be devoted to direct evaluation. Students need to be observed while they are trying to engage in instructional activities. It is indeed unfortunate that time and place set aside for students to engage in these activities are isolated from a teacher's direct observation. Much of this work is given as homework assignments or relegated to study halls. This work is too important to be done outside the range of the evaluative eye of the teacher. More will be said about the issue of homework in a later chapter.

Teachers need to spend far more time observing and evaluating and less time in what we usually consider teaching. The assessment dimension that is outlined here is far too important a part of instruction to be so much ignored. This activity is not currently done with any great frequency; it couldn't be, because most evaluation is primarily directed to giving grades.

There is another important reason for using instruction as assessment. It is the best means of finding out if a student really does have a learning handicap. When students are given work that is too difficult for them, it is not possible to tell if their off-task behavior is the result of the task difficulty or the result of some disability which is internal to the student. The only way to determine if the cause of a learning problem is in the student or in the instructional activity given to the student is to change the learning activity to match the student's need. If when given work that is carefully prepared to produce scores in the success range the student still demonstrates excessive off-task behavior, then the odds are very good this student has a significant learning disability. Checking to see if there is residual off-task behavior after providing appropriate instructional level activities is the most valid way of identifying real learning disabilities. Students so identified need and should qualify for special education services. They are not simply curriculum casualties.

Special education has come under considerable criticism in recent years, because there doesn't seem to be anything special about what it does with learning disabled students. The observation is correct that special educators don't use any special instructional material or methods with most of their students; they really don't need them. The only thing special they typically do is identify regular activities and materials that individual students can do. These materials and activities are simply from a lower level of difficulty than the regular classroom teachers are able or willing to use. The observation is correct that much of what special educators do is not a lot different, but the criticism is unfair.

The pressure to give grades in special classrooms is eliminated. When a student is doing poorly on an activity, the activity is likely to be changed. The student's performance on an activity is the focal point for change in instructional activity.

In primary grades, oral reading activities are common, and oral reading performance is commonly used to evaluate reading skill. Oral reading is a central measure of reading ability. Remember the reading levels described by Betts (1946). These standards should be used to adjust the difficulty of reading material so that students demonstrate oral reading behavior that is at the instructional level. If a student cannot identify more than 4 percent of the words in the material he is required to read, then new material should be provided for the student so that he can readily identify at least 96 percent of the words. Also, if a student's comprehension of material being read falls below 75 percent, then select other material which is not as difficult. Both of these indexes—number of unknown words and level of comprehension—should be considered when listening to a child reading orally.

This does not mean that each word a child can't identify is noted and percentages calculated everytime a child reads orally. It means that the teacher is attending to this performance informally to see if the child has difficulty with more than about one word in every other sentence. It means that the teacher is aware that a student is having difficulty answering basic questions about a selection he has just read. These are the informal assessment probes that the teacher must always be using when listening to students reading. If at this very informal level the child is showing problems, then a closer look is warranted. If the material does, indeed, exceed the instructional level bounds, then get reading material that does fit the student.

When students are reading silently, signs of frustration or off-task behavior should be noted. If students demonstrate these behaviors, then a closer look is warranted. If the material proves to be too difficult, adjust the difficulty level.

A cautionary note is in order when using oral reading to assess the instructional level match. It is a good idea to let the student read through material silently before he is required to read it aloud. A student should not be required to cope with problems of pronunciation and comprehension simultaneously. Also, the fluency and rate of oral reading is normally quite varied among individuals. Fluency may also be influenced by having to perform in front of others. Most attention should be given to the number of unknown words a student is encountering. Best evidence of an unknown word occurs when a student simply refuses to say it or obviously mispronounces it.

It is not necessary to use detailed informal assessment procedures when observing a student's oral reading. The signs of frustration level reading are obvious. These are the signs a teacher must watch for as reading instruction proceeds. This is the basic assessment procedure to use in reading instruction when students are actually reading.

When reading material is the medium of instruction, the match between instructional level and student should be judged by the same informal procedures as for reading instruction. Now, however, the comprehension check serves the dual function of determining both the appropriateness of the reading level as well as the amount of information on the subject area gained while reading. Certainly, if the subject area reading material is so difficult that the student does not gain the essential information from reading it, a change in the material is in order. The questions to be answered or exercises to be performed following any reading activity should be scored with these uses in mind. Above 70 percent correct is necessary for reading appropriateness, and that score or better if the student is to make the most of using it in learning content from the subject area.

Make sure that no more new information, i.e. spelling words, subtraction facts, names of presidents, etc., is given at one time than a student can get correct in drill and seatwork activities. Good performance and accuracy are important in drill. If a student is missing a third of his spelling words on the weekly test, it means that he should be getting a shorter list to practice on at the beginning of the week. He is practicing too many different words. He probably could get more of the words correct if he had simply been given fewer to begin with. Give the student no more words to study than he will get with near complete accuracy with the allotted practice time.

In summary, assessment should be an integral component of instruction. Regular kinds of scoring can be used but with the idea of adjusting the instructional activity or material to produce scores that indicate the instructional level has been attained.

Chapter 12

THE STUDENT-CENTERED CURRICULUM

L ow achieving students are in trouble, because they seldom find places on the curriculum where they can achieve. Disadvantaged students are in still more difficulty because of missing skills which are prerequisite to performance on curricular activities.

Wherever the students are placed, no matter if they are retained, the curriculum moves on. These students cannot keep pace. They fail. They don't achieve. They drop out.

The curriculum is tied to a rigid structure. The schools' calendar and its sequence of grades define the structure. We try to fit students to the structure of the curriculum by grouping and tracking, failing and promoting. Since we try to fit such a diverse group of students to a fixed structure, we invariably have casualties.

Does our instructional delivery system need to be changed? It is unlikely that major changes in this system will be forthcoming. However, changes in this system are desperately needed to prevent the failure and the forcing out of low achieving and disadvantaged students.

How much change in the system is needed? The answer to this question depends on the answer to another question. How many students are failing and dropping out? The answer to the first question is that the system needs at least as much change as necessary to successfully handle the students who are failing and dropping out.

The dropout rate is quite varied from school to school, school system to school system. More change is needed where the problems are greater.

What is the change that is needed? Fundamentally, it is this: We must stop trying to fit low achieving and disadvantaged students into the curriculum structure; we must fit the curriculum to them. Think of it this way: A student is placed on his personal curricular course. It need not be any different than the standard curriculum. His starting place on

84

it is identified, and he is permitted to work along this course at a rate at which he can succeed and achieve.

This rate will be different than that required by a curriculum assigned to school structures of grades and calendars. Here the student must march in lock-step along with other students. If his ability level is different, he will falter, fail, and fall behind. If, on the other hand, the curriculum is assigned to the student, he can march at his own pace. The confirmed institutionalized system of assigning curriculum to grades, not students, makes the needed change difficult.

It is difficult to imagine both systems coexisting in the school, let alone the same classroom. Can it be done with some of the students without having to change the whole system? We know that students can be assigned their own curriculum in segregated settings where the teacher must deal, as a matter of fact, with multiple differences. Special classes and resource rooms are examples of its occurrence in special education. Multiple grade classrooms in rural schools are examples in regular education. These structures are administrative and practical. These kinds of structures and changes will be discussed in a later chapter. Here the discussion will focus on assigning the curriculum to students, or making the curriculum student-centered.

Administrative restructuring of the entire system would certainly facilitate the change to a student-centered curriculum. Even without such a great change, it is within the power of individual teachers to make this change in their classroom. After all, it is the individual teacher who most feels the effect of the mismatch between student and curriculum.

It is within the classroom teacher's power to make the curriculum student-centered for the low achieving and disadvantaged students. The argument, or question, that often arises about doing this concerns what happens when these students leave classrooms where the curriculum is student-centered and move back to classrooms where the curriculum is lock-step. The response is that we owe these students our best effort while we have them. They deserve the same success experiences as the majority of students. We can only hope to solve the problem of non-achievement and dropouts by making a start at making the curriculum student-centered.

The first step in making a curriculum student-centered is to find out where a given student can function best on the curriculum. In order to do this, much of the curriculum should be viewed as a test. In those curricular areas with detailed scope and sequence of skills such as reading and math, inventories can be constructed from them. Such inventories are occassionally a part of commercial reading and math programs. These tests are given to the student, and the threshold or entry level of the student is determined. The entry level is the place where a student demonstrates mastery over the majority of the preceding items on the curriculum. It is his readiness base. This is especially important to identify if the curricular items are in a skills hierarchy. In other words, are the items in a readiness relationship to each other. The lower-placed items are prerequisite to those that follow. The whole mathematics curriculum is more highly ordered in this regard. Some science curricula have readiness relationships with math curricula as well. The students readiness position is his entry position. Also, any noted deficits should be considered as high priority for teaching. The deficits in the readiness base will affect the progress at the entry level if they are not remedied.

An overriding entry skill is the students' reading ability. Print is the primary medium for instruction in all curricular areas. The students need at least the level of reading skill required of the instructional materials used in any subject area. If the student has sufficient readiness skill to cope with the content but not sufficient reading skill to gain access to the content through print, some adjustments are in order. The teacher will have to find printed material which presents the desired content but with a reading level within the student's threshold. The other option is to find non-print means of presenting the content.

After entry level has been determined, movement along the curriculum is determined by mastery of each step. Has the student clearly achieved the curricular objectives at the point of entry?

Time to mastery will be greater for most of these students. Regular curricular material provides introduction rates, practice, and pace which are quicker than the needs of low achieving students. These students will require the additional time and repetition it takes for them to demonstrate success and mastery.

The students' individual capacity for new items will dictate the pace of each to a certain extent. The remainder of the pace will be governed by their individual need for repetition and practice. What is the instructional burden that a student can carry efficiently and successfully? This question ultimately is determined by observing the students' performance while engaged in a learning activity. Introduction and repetition rates constitute the burden. The need for adjustments in these are necessary for low achieving students. Place of introduction, amount introduced, and amount of repetition are all governed by the curriculum structure.

The distribution of these is fixed in place. It is largely predetermined. It is the lock-step so frequently mentioned.

The place of introduction of a new skill should be determined by the student's level of achievement, by testing his skill level. The amount to be introduced must be determined by the student's own performance. What is the maximum number of new items that can be introduced to a student that can be retained successfully and practiced accurately? How much repetition does the student need once he reaches the practice stage? This is answered with another question which requires observation to answer. How many times does an item have to be practiced before it is retained with some permanence?

The different needs of low achieving and disadvantaged students requires a flexible curriculum that can be made to fit them. They certainly can't be made plastic to fit a rigid curricular structure.

The details of repetition and introduction requirements will be discussed in later chapters where the teaching of subject matter is discussed. In general terms, though, low achieving students may require as much as twice the practice that average students require. This is particularly true at beginning levels of instruction. For example, when children are first learning to recognize words, the average student will need about 35 repetitions of a word before he can recognize the word instantly. More specifically stated, an average student must correctly identify an unfamiliar word 35 times before it becomes completely familiar and instantly recognizable (Gates, 1930; Hargis, 1982, 1987; Hargis et al., 1988). Some children require many fewer repetitions; some require many more. Reading curricular materials provides adequate repetition for most students. However, it is inadequate for low achieving students (Hargis, 1987).

A student should have assigned to him the necessary curricular space as well as instructional materials to get the necessary repetition he needs to achieve mastery. Individual curricular assignment permits this space and time to vary. It also permits a student to enter at a point where he is clearly ready.

Movement along the curriculum is determined by mastery of previous objectives. The readiness base is built of mastered steps on the curriculum. This is an important notion. A student's entry point is based on what he can do. It is based on known or mastered skills. This requires a necessary change in focus of assessment. What a student knows or can do becomes more important than what he can't do or what his deficiencies are.

Assigning the curriculum to the student requires this change in emphasis in assessment.

Finding what a student can do and what he has mastered permits a far more meaningful approach to reporting achievement. The focus of evaluation can move from grades to real substantive reports of progress. The specific statements of what a student has achieved and what a student is learning on his curriculum is far more meaningful than an abstract grade or percentile rank. This kind of report can also permit continuity in instruction from one teacher or class to the next. The next teacher will be specifically aware of where to take up appropriate instructional activity with a particular student.

Chapter 13

MEASURING PROGRESS WITHOUT GRADES

Achievement progress is not really measured with grades. A letter grade or a percentage grade is only an abstraction. It tells nothing of the specifics learned or not learned. Letter grades are often calculated from distributions of scores. Letter grades derived in such a manner only show performance relative to others doing the same work. Grades given in one school or school system may not be equivalent to the grades given in another. A letter grade of "C" given to a student in a class composed of academically talented students does not mean the same thing in terms of achievement as a "C" given to a student in the same course but in a class composed of more typical students.

Grades at the end of grading periods may be averages of other grades. If they are, they give no specific information concerning what the student learned or where the student ended on the curricular ladder. A student whose performance was lower at the beginning and higher at the end of the grading period may actually have achieved far more than a student in the opposite situation, yet both students may receive the same final grade.

Reasonable progress reports should focus on ultimate achievement outcomes. This is the information that is needed for maintaining continuity of appropriate instruction and effective transition from point to point on the curriculum. The specifics of what a student can do are needed for structuring activities that produce success and achievement.

Other grading systems report the percent correct on tests that sample items taken from instruction. Again, these percentages may be averaged over a grading period. Curricular items mastered at the end of the grading period then are weighted no more heavily than those mastered at the beginning. This information may be somewhat more specific than letter grades, in that it indicates, to some extent, the percentage correct on tests of the curriculum.

Either of the above systems are fundamentally ineffective, often destructive, procedures for reporting progress for low achieving and disadvantaged students. What is useful information about progress is the specific detailed measurement of the mastery of objectives along the curriculum sequence. This information provides several components necessary for successful instructional planning. It tells where to start instruction and what materials are appropriate for use with the student. The best approach to this is actually using the instructional material as the test material. The level of material where the student shows good performance—the instructional level—is the entry point or readiness level. Measuring specific items learned may be necessary if individual material must be prepared.

In any case, this specific information provides far better information about progress or achievement than does a letter grade or a score. An instructional reading level is far more specific in regard to achievement. It tells precisely at what level a student is able to read. It can tell specifically what the student is working on. This information is not only useful in reports of progress, but it is also the necessary information for instruction. It provides readiness or entry level information. It provides the specific information needed to structure individual instructional level material. It shows what is next to be presented.

Measurement effort should be directed to this instructional matching process; it is a measurement process that should replace measurement for grades. The two approaches to assessment are polar opposites. They are antithetical. The two approaches cannot legitimately coexist.

Measurement of mastery and the instructional match are far more helpful in gauging the amount of achievement progress over time. A "D" at the beginning and the end of the year tells nothing of what has been learned. Norm-referenced achievement tests can do better. They may sample only a few things that come from the curriculum being used, but that may be sufficient to mark the progress a student or group of students make over time. Better measures are made up of the curriculum being used. What has been taught is being tested. The validity of the measurement is assured, and real change can be judged specifically and objectively. The validity of the report of progress is also assured. What was learned is reported.

Even though the curriculum-based measures of progress mentioned above are valid and substantive, grades are an institution; they are expected. Giving substantive reports of progress will not always satisfy the need for seeing a letter grade. Parents especially may feel the need to see grades for their children. They want to know how their children are doing comparatively. In these cases normative information can satisfy the need for comparative information. There are several measures that can be used to provide this information. A student's instructional reading level is a concrete index of how a student is doing relative to grade placement and other students in his classroom. The instructional reading level is a grade level number that is itself a normative index based on grade sequence. The instructional reading level is the grade level equivalent of the most difficult book a student can read with at least 75 percent comprehension and in which 96 percent of the words are familiar. If a student achieves these percentages in a fifth grade reader, for example, then his instructional reading level could be reported as being at the fifth grade level. It is nearly impossible to further assign a grade to the instructional reading level, since the performance criteria for achieving it is the same for everyone regardless of the grade level indicated. It is an objective means of reporting performance. It gives a concrete indication of achievement and it gives normative information. Given this index, parents can compare their children's performance with others in their grade or age group.

The curriculum-based inventories that should be used to trace achievement along the curriculum should also be used to report progress to parents. From these, parents can get the specific information about what has been learned, and they can also compare their children's place on the curricular sequence to that of their grade and age-mates.

The comparative aspect of this information will not be particularly pertinent to teachers. There are exceptions, however. Teachers should be interested in comparing student progress over time. They should compare student achievement to their potential for achievement; they should compare the progress of their students to similar students in the larger population.

Reports of progress are basically of two types. One form is normative and the other substantive. The normative reports are those that compare a student or students to some standard. The standard is represented by a norm or average. Each grade number represents the average performance of the students in that grade. The grade number is assigned to performance in reading, math, social studies, or any content subject area that makes up the curriculum. Standardized tests are also analyzed to produce grade level equivalents for any score obtained. Grade level scores have become a common form of reporting achievement test scores. Grade level equivalents are easy to understand.

Books and instructional reading materials are also evaluated to determine their grade level difficulty. This evaluation can be done directly by checking the performance of students in different grades while reading the material. More often, the material is evaluated by readability formulas which attempt to do the same thing. These formulas are designed to check the difficulty of the language by examining the vocabulary difficulty and sentence complexity (Hargis, 1982). These formulas are helpful, but they do not have nearly the precision of the direct measure of readability. There is a considerable error of measurement in readability formulas. So when determining students' instructional reading level by letting them read material which has been graded by formula, the grade level assigned to each book or selection may not be precisely accurate.

All of the normative types of reports or indexes are fairly imprecise. This imprecision is more troublesome at the primary grade levels when the information is used to make instructional decisions.

Substantive evaluation yields information on the specifics of what has been learned and where a student is working on the curriculum. The result of this assessment is not an abstraction; it is not a numeric value or a letter. The results are usually a direct statement of what the student has learned. For example, rather than saying a student can read at the second grade level, the name would be provided of the specific book the student had completed or was reading in. In math, the specific addition or multiplication facts mastered would be reported instead of reporting a grade on a test of such facts.

Normative reports are needed, even demanded by some parents. Substantive reports are necessary for use by teachers. Teachers need information on where a student is on the continuum of items and objectives that make up the curriculum. This information tells the teacher what a student needs to be doing. It also shows where a student is most likely to fit with success. A teacher needs substantive information to see if students are mastering the objectives as well as working at instructional levels. This information needs to be collected directly and regularly by observing the performance of the students and checking their work. Substantive information needs to be used in transition situations. When students transfer from one school or school system to another, substantive information is helpful in placing the new students appropriately. When a student changes from one teacher to the next through promotion or mainstreaming, continuity and success for the student is preserved through substantive measures of student progress.

The higher the achievement levels a student has attained, the more normative the reports can be when transition situations occur. At the primary grade levels of achievement particularly, it is very easy to put a student in a failure situation. For example, saying that a student can read at the primer level does not mean that he can be placed in any basal reader's primer and read at an instructional level. There simply is not sufficient precision in this normative information. Primer level books vary remarkably from one series to the next in terms of vocabulary. The ability to read in one does not mean the student can read in all or any of the others at an instructional level. In fact the low achieving student is very likely to find frustration in reading the others. More substance needs to be in the report. Which primer a student can read in, what sight words he has acquired, and which word identification skills a student has learned would constitute helpful information that could make a successful transition.

Normative information becomes more usable at the higher achievement levels. Reporting that a student can read instructionally at the sixth grade level is useful information to another teacher. When a student attains more substantial reading ability, grade level skill designations can predict with good certainty that a student will be able to read other materials that are at that level. Certainly the report of reading levels above primary grades can suggest thresholds or error margins that teachers should not exceed in finding a starting place where students can work successfully.

A final comment concerning norm-referenced achievement tests is in order. There has been recent criticism of such tests because of the norms themselves. These tests are given to populations of students to check the performance of students on the tests. The normative scores for the students subsequently given these tests are determined by comparing their performance to data gained by giving the test to the standardization population. The criticism of the tests concerns this. Students currently being given these tests are doing better than the norms would indicate. In other words, average scores are higher than the average scores in the norms. This itself would not seem to be a controversial issue. It would simply suggest that the educational system is doing better by the students. The problem with a majority of students doing above average is that as a practical matter this can't happen. That is, average performance is really determined on the spot. Average performance is determined by calculating the arithmetic mean from the group of students in question. However, we must remember that norms are established on particular populations at a particular date. Critics apparently have forgotten this fact. We should always remember this information when comparing student performance to norms.

Actually, having dated norms is a good idea. We should not be without such standards. Being without them would be like determining the value of the dollar without having historic dates for determining values. We can compare today's dollar value with its value in numerous past years. This permits us to judge the effects of economic policies, business cycles, social upheavals, etc. Having dated achievement norms permits the study of changing curriculum, methods, technology, educational policy, teacher education, etc.

If we constantly change norms and tests without keeping such benchmarks, we will lose valuable research data and we will continually frustrate ourselves. We will not know if we are actually improving in a larger sense if we can only compare ourselves with ourselves at that moment. Certainly, we can continue to compare individuals with the current norms or compare one subpopulation with others that are similar. Without dated norms, however, we lose the ability to measure progress or achievement in the instructional delivery system itself. We can't check the effect of instruction over time unless we have the same test with the norms that were used at the beginning of the time period being studied.

Changing norms may make us feel like we are on a treadmill and going nowhere. Actually, we need both new norms and old norms. However, to keep old norms we must be willing to leave the tests pretty much unchanged or keep them as similar as possible. We should not be so ready to change tests by abandoning test items just because too many students are getting them correct. Wouldn't that simply mean that the students were learning the skills or information sampled by those items?

Some critics will say reflexively that improvement in test scores is due to the fact that the teachers are teaching the test. One wonders how we could conclude otherwise. Tests are supposed to measure what is being taught. If the teaching of this content is good, test scores go up. If the teaching is poor, test scores go down. The critics should be reminded of what makes a test valid. Tests should measure what is being taught. This is an essential ingredient in the validity of achievement tests. The fact is we should always be teaching to tests. Perhaps a better way of stating that is, we should always be testing what we teach. Tests and instruction must have this intimate relationship if the relationship is to be productive.

At any rate, without having some tests that have norms with dates in the past, it is not possible to adequately judge the progress of groups of students over time.

There are a variety of reasons for measuring progress. There are a variety of means to do so usefully. Some are substantive; some are normative. However, none of the useful procedures involves the giving of grades.

Chapter 14

COOPERATIVE LEARNING

A substantial body of literature supporting cooperative learning activities has accumulated over the past 16 years (Topping, 1988; Uttero, 1988; Stevens et al., 1987; Slavin, 1987, 1983; Glasser, 1986). In general the system involves placing students in four- to five-member groups of mixed ability. After initial instruction by the teacher, the students work together cooperatively on worksheets or other practice materials until each student in the group gets the correct answers. The students discuss the answers, reach consensus, drill each other, and assess one another to make certain that each group member will demonstrate mastery when assessed individually by the teacher. The students' scores on these individual assessments are summed to form group or team scores. These scores are used to provide recognition to the team.

The success of the team requires cooperation. There is an incentive for all students to do well and for all students to help their teammates. As students provide one another with explanations of concepts or skills, they themselves gain in achievement. This cycle of cooperative learning significantly increases student achievement.

There are several significant components of the cooperative learning approach that are important for use with low achieving and disadvantaged students. The cooperative, rather than competitive, orientation is very important. Low achieving and disadvantaged students are, almost by definition, unable to compete in regular school programs. Competition for them means coming in last and getting failing grades. In cooperative learning programs, all students must perform well. It is the role of each student to assist each of the other students in learning and performing well. No one is to fail; no one is to come in last. Also, in the act of assisting each other, learning is further enhanced in the helper.

Cooperation rather than competition has direct benefits aside from achievement gains for students. When the teacher and students expect everyone to be doing well and everyone cooperates with each other in doing this, chronic failure experience is eliminated. With this, the students' feelings of self-esteem and confidence can reach normal levels. An environment where all students are expected and assisted to do well is a place where a student can feel accepted and secure. Cooperative learning arrangements make mentally healthy environments for students.

A truly significant component of cooperative learning arrangements is the change in quality and focus on what have been called "follow-up" activities. In traditional elementary reading instruction, one of the most common features is the use of reading groups (Hiebert, 1983). The typical procedure when working with reading groups is that while the teacher is working with one reading group the other students in the other groups are working on activities that take little teacher supervision. These are the "follow-up" activities. Research on these follow-up activities suggests that they are often of poor quality. They are seldom integrated with the other reading activities, and the time on-task during follow-up activities is quite low (Stevens et al., 1987). Moreover, about two-thirds of reading time is spent on follow-up activities in a room with three reading groups.

In a cooperative learning arrangement, the follow-up time becomes the central focus of activity. The quality of the follow-up time is the most important part of reading instruction. This is the largest segment of time devoted to reading instruction, and that time is effective engaged time. Achievement is a function of the amount of academically engaged time. Students in four- or five-member teams can be engaged and assisted far more extensively in any activity than they can as part of a ten- or twenty-five-member group. In the cooperative setting, the student who is assisting is also benefitting from engaged time in the activity.

The quality of engaged time is enhanced because of the immediate and constant feedback each student gets. As important, each student must get everything correct. Most drill activities occur in follow-up time. The quality of drill is greatly enhanced in a cooperative setting. Drill is only beneficial when the student gets things correct at the majority of repetitions. Correctness, getting things right, is a purpose of cooperative activity.

Teacher-centered instruction is reduced and student-engaged time is increased. When the teacher is responsible for directing and orchestrating all the instructional activities, students waste much of the day. Thurlow et al. (1984) found that the average second grade student reads aloud 90 seconds per day. Most oral reading takes place in reading groups where the students who are waiting their turn to read may be wasting time. Certainly, if the reading material is above their instructional reading level, a great deal of time will be wasted.

The cooperative learning approach is student-centered. This places the primary emphasis on the so-called "follow-up" activities. The four-or five-member teams permit far more time to be spent engaged in learning. Even when students are involved in checking or assessing fellow students' work they are engaged, and they are gaining practice leading to mastery and fluency.

Another important feature is the fact that each student is to reach an acceptable performance criterion in each activity. The emphasis is changed to succeeding. The monitoring and checking done by team members is done to make sure that each student is getting things right. Students can get immediate feedback on performance. Errors are corrected immediately. The opportunity to practice errors can be greatly reduced. The checking that is done during these cooperative activities is not for assigning grades. It is done to head off further errors and insure that practice leads to the desired performance criterion. Grading is not involved in this kind of assessment.

Children who fail in the competitive grade-oriented classrooms need a cooperative learning approach to keep them from becoming casualties. Competition is only motivating for those students who have sufficient skill and ability to be competitive. Grades are only motivating to those students who can get good grades. In competitive instructional programs, low achieving students, by definition, always finish last. It is demoralizing for them.

In competitive environments, when students realize there is little hope for doing well, there is a strong temptation to cheat. There is little temptation to cheat when everyone is supposed to do well. All students should get all they do correct. Cooperative learning arrangements benefit low achieving and disadvantaged students. Cheating will not be troublesome. Furthermore, students will not be demonstrating other problem behaviors, learned because of their inability to be competitive and then frustration from failure.

Cooperative learning procedures can make all students effective learners. Not all learners operate at the same efficiency level, however. Some low achievers vary considerably from their age and grade peers in achievement level and learning rate. If the curriculum is assigned to grade levels in lock-step, even cooperative learning arrangements may have their beneficial characteristics nullified. If all the students are required to perform at grade level rather than their individual instructional level, there will be fewer benefits gained from cooperative learning arrangements.

Combining cooperative learning with curriculum-based assessment procedures will provide both benefits. Students can work cooperatively at their individual instructional levels and rates. Cooperative learning procedures and curriculum-based assessment are entirely compatible in regard to their designed purposes; success for all students is a central focus. The importance of academically engaged time is emphasized. Instructional activity itself is used as the focus of assessment.

Cooperative learning strategies organize the system of delivery of instruction; curriculum-based assessment procedures define the criteria to be used in all phases of assessment. Curriculum-based assessment provides the criteria for the teacher to use in making decisions about entry levels, instructional levels, and mastery. It provides the performance criteria for the student team members to check during the ongoing activities while students are engaged in follow-up activities.

Both of these systems have demonstrated their effectiveness. They both should be incorporated in the education of low achieving and disadvantaged students.

Combining the two systems has some mutually enhancing benefits. The competitive aspect of assessment is virtually eliminated by using curriculum-based assessment. Progress is not reported through grades. There is even less pressure to cheat. All measurement becomes a routine part of instruction and it is not threatening. Students are only supposed to do as well as they can and are supposed to get all their work correct, and the system is set up to make sure that they do.

There are other ways in which the educational system can behave in more cooperative ways to enhance the achievement of low achieving and disadvantaged students. Teachers can act cooperatively. There is actually a great deal of overlap in the achievement levels of students from one grade to the next. Yet, the boundaries between grades are sharply drawn in the lock-step. Teachers may feel an isolated duty to their place on the curriculum. The fact that some students don't fit is not the teachers' responsibility; it is the responsibility of some specialist who handles such things. This attitude results from the relative isolation that each grade has.

The barriers that isolate the grades should be broken down by cooperative effort among teachers. Teachers should plan for cooperative learning activities for students of overlapping abilities between the grade levels. This would permit a cooperative continuum of instruction that would let students work at different paces. When such cooperative arrangements are organized by teachers, many of the destructive effects of the lock-step are removed.

Such arrangements among teachers permit them to maintain contact with students for a longer time. Cooperation facilitates transition, and the longer contact and greater familiarity with students' performance helps still more.

The specialization of teachers has caused still more isolation and reduced cooperation. Teachers are trained and employed as specialists. At the elementary levels it is by grades and at the secondary levels it becomes increasingly tied to subject areas. This contributes to the most destructive problems of the lock-step at the secondary level.

Armies of students march through the specialist's room each day. A specialist may see 150 or more different students in a day's time. The specialist may alone be responsible for teaching a particular subject. There may be virtually no opportunity to engage in cooperative activities with other teachers. With individual students, there is little opportunity to do more than score papers to give grades. Students pass in and out of the specialist's doors in lock-step. Those who can't remain in step fail and drop out. These teachers deal with too many different students to consider individual differences or readily engage the students in cooperative activities. The specialist may have a student for no more than one subject for one year. The mix of students in the specialist's room changes each hour. The opportunity to become familiar with individual students is limited. In one week, if class time were divided equally among students, only about ten minutes of individual attention could be given to each of 125 different students. Teachers end up spending more out-of-class time grading papers of the students. However, the classroom is the place where it is possible for a teacher to directly observe (and check) a student's performance in ongoing instructional activity. Two minutes per student per class could be devoted to direct observation, if the class time were totally devoted to it. This small amount of time might be sufficient if the teacher's organizational skill was superb and the instructional routine did not require other kinds of activities.

Cooperative learning activities and curriculum-based assessment are possible in such situations, though it is apparent that such organization around specialists encourages a lock-step approach. Cooperative learning and curriculum-based assessment work best in situations where teachers deal with fewer students for longer periods of time. If a teacher has the same twenty-five students for the whole day, the two minutes per day per student becomes ten minutes per day of potential observation and assessment time. The disruption of class changes each period is greatly reduced. A teacher can become much more familiar with an individual student's performance and his instructional needs. Individual attention can be used much more efficiently. The teacher can devote more and more time to planning and the preparation and selection of materials. Cooperative teamwork activities will engage the student for most of the school day.

Teachers who enter cooperative arrangements with other teachers can gain still more time for planning and materials preparation. Two or more teachers, working cooperatively, can and do plan time for preparation and planning. When curriculum-based assessment is used, a teacher's preparation and planning time must increase as the information gained from ongoing assessment is translated into instructional materials and activities for individual students.

Cooperation among teachers can increase the array of materials available. Multilevels of materials will be necessary to match students' needs. If teachers over two or more grade levels cooperate, the levels of materials available for each will naturally increase as their resources are combined. This could easily be accomplished at the elementary level. The access to more levels of curricular activity is extremely important when curriculum-based assessment is used.

With the wider range of materials and the overlapping range of ability levels in the combined classes, student teams can encompass different ability levels more effectively. Transition is smoothed; teachers remain in contact with the same students for two or more years.

Teachers vary in skills and talents. Cooperative arrangements bring these variable abilities together to the students' benefit.

Rasinski (1988) points out that teachers tend to isolate students communicatively and physically. They are constantly prompted to work alone, work quietly, stop chattering. The environment is often competitive. The students are isolated from social interaction and placed in intensive competition with each other. Students are urged to be a "winner," to be "number one." Scores and accumulated points are graphically displayed to show the relative standings. Resinski feels that it is difficult for children to learn citizenship and cooperation when the teacher turns the classroom community into a classroom of isolated individuals. Each individual is learning to seek her or his own personal gain at the expense of others. In the competitive environment, children are given strong signals that cooperation and helping others are not important parts of the classroom community or the community that exists outside of school.

I believe competitive classroom environments help foster the notion that it is alright for some students to fail. If there are winners, there must be losers. The competitive, isolated organization must change to an environment emphasizing cooperation. All students would benefit, but it is an essential change if low achieving and disadvantaged students are to be treated fairly.

Schools that have practiced cooperative learning of some kind or another are not new. What is new is that the cooperative learning activities are being introduced into large comprehensive schools with many tracks and ability groups.

Cooperative learning has never ceased in the remaining rural and isolated school systems with small student populations. For example, Stony Fork School in Campbell County, Tennessee is the smallest comprehensive school in the state. The school has 83 students in thirteen grades, including kindergarten. Each teacher in the school is responsible for three grades. The principal, also a teacher at the high school level, teaches every subject to the 24 high school students. This includes algebra, economics, Spanish, history, and English.

Cooperative learning occurs in settings like these. Teachers that have kindergarten through second or third grade levels are virtually compelled to use it. Teachers know their students very well in classrooms like these. Students progress along the curriculum and proceed, of necessity, at their own pace. The students don't change teachers every year. The teacher simply continues the work uninterrupted by grade change. In these classrooms there is constant contact with the curriculum both above and below a student's present working location. Students are not placed in isolation at one spot in the curriculum. Teachers have constant contact with students through several levels of work. Readiness is enhanced through familiarity. Students engaging in tutoring or collaborating learn through the elaborated explanations and assistance they provide. Cooperative work is the norm.

Large schools have organizations that encourage increasingly narrow specialization around limited pieces of the curriculum. Students are isolated; cooperation is stifled. I recommend such small school organizations be applied in large comprehensive schools.

Chapter 15

READING AND WRITING

Language

By the time most children start school, they have mastered the language of their place of birth. They have the ability to engage in conversation with their peers or adults. The principle limitation to their range of conversation will be their vocabulary development. All the grammatical forms of the language will have been mastered.

The acquisition of language is a normal process and occurs without conscious effort, even though the process is a remarkably complex one. However, it is so commonplace an occurrence its complexity goes unnoted except by a few linguists who study it. The process is entirely implicit. Children have no conscious knowledge of the details of what they are learning or even the fact that they are learning anything. Learning the written form of the language is a different matter. It requires gaining some conscious, explicit knowledge of language. The problem of gaining this explicit knowledge produces a good deal of the difficulty many low achieving students have in learning to read and write.

Most children have mastered the language by the time they are required to start learning to read and write it. If there is a deficit in language experience during the preschool years, or if the language experience is primarily in another language, children will have difficulty learning to read and write.

Most children have learned the essential features of the language by the time they begin school. However, age of mastery of this language readiness base is normally varied. Age six is average, but normal children achieve the same stage of language readiness earlier or later. The children who achieve it at a later age will have difficulty if they begin instruction at age six. Mastery of the essential features of language is a necessary readiness base for beginning to learn to read and write. These features include all its grammatical forms and a stock of common vocabulary. Again, this knowledge is implicit; it is learned without conscious awareness or effort.

In reading, a child will need to learn the unfamiliar printed form of words that are familiar in their spoken form. They will be making conscious effort to learn the unfamiliar printed form. If the language represented in print is also unfamiliar, the learning process is blocked. A basic readiness requirement for learning to read is: only the printed form of the language should be unfamiliar. The language of beginning reading materials should be familiar if read aloud to students for whom it is intended.

Language has two fundamental dimensions. It is both received and expressed. It must be comprehended and produced. Listening and reading are receptive. Speaking and writing are expressive. Listening comprehension of language is necessary in order to learn to read it. The requirements for learning to write a language are more complex. Normally, you must be able to produce a language through speech before you can write it. However, you must be able to read the language as well. One must be familiar with the printed form of the language before one can write it. One cannot write more or better than one can read. Most certainly, however, there is no assurance that most will be able to write as well as they read. For example, the ability to read and comprehend Shakespeare in no way suggests that the reader could produce similar written work. Writing has a more complex readiness base than reading. Writing requires handwriting and spelling ability. These two are the most obvious characteristics of written language. However, written expression requires composition skills. Sentences must be composed and discourse must be organized.

Reading is like following a map. Writing is like drawing a map. With any given map, the skills required to prepare it are greater than those required to follow it. Likewise, the relation exists between reading and writing. The skills required to write a given selection are greater than those required to read the selection. Writing requires reading, but it requires, also, the additional layer of compositional skills and abilities.

The ability to write skillfully is quite variable. Literary talent is rare. Even the ability to write stories that children enjoy is not commonplace. However, there is a basal set of functional writing skills that are teachable and learnable. Low achieving students can learn to summarize and describe events in their lives. They can learn to prepare a coherent set of directions. Critics may say that such objectives are too modest. Still, I believe that the difficulty of teaching the written form of language is not understood. Consequently, low achieving students don't acquire this skill. I believe in formulating reasonably attainable objectives that will make students succeed. In the atmosphere of accomplishment, skill and talent differences can emerge, and all students can acquire at least functional skill.

Reading

Instruction in reading is fruitless unless a child is ready to learn. The principle readiness requirement for learning to read is language readiness. A child cannot follow the teacher's verbal directions or understand printed language if that language is not as yet familiar. The language may be unfamiliar to the student, because he has simply not reached the required level of maturity. Reading instruction should not be started until children reach the language readiness threshold required.

The typical kindergarten teacher is probably quite aware of which students are not ready for beginning reading instruction. This awareness comes from the informal observation of children in daily activities. Some children will obviously not be ready. They can't follow verbal directions well and may not be able to understand some instruction at all. They appear bored or inattentive when being read to. Most of these children only need more time. They can't be hurried along. Kindergarten should be an open-ended period for them. They need sufficient time in a language-rich, but unstructured environment so that they can demonstrate the necessary language-readiness base that will permit them comfort and success in beginning reading.

Remember, language is learned unconsciously and implicitly. It is not learned in a structured environment. It is learned by playing and squabbling with other children and through informal, daily interaction with adults. With the disadvantaged student, the preschool time is very important. The preschool and kindergarten will provide the language experience environment that is needed for understanding the language of print and instruction. This experience will augment a poor or inadequate experience in the home environment or supplant the experience of the children whose home language is other than English.

Disadvantaged children need experience with books. Books or any reading material may be missing from their experience. Some language experiences are gained only by being read to. Some language structures, especially the direct discourse form, is largely a device of printed language. It is the means by which conversation is represented in print (Hargis, 1982). The altered word order and added syntactic complexity cause confusion if the student is not familiar with it. Conversation represented by direct quotation is the most common grammatical form in beginning basal readers (Hargis, 1974). Students need familiarity with this and other conventions of printed language. The only way a student can gain this familiarity is by being read to. Reading aloud to low achieving and disadvantaged students is a very basic and important readiness activity.

Language readiness is, of course, the most direct requirement for beginning reading, but students also need physical and social maturity sufficient to participate in the structured activities of beginning reading. In the United States we are in a rush to begin reading instruction. In European schools, the students may not begin reading instruction until about age seven (Wham, 1987). This would be a very beneficial change for low achieving students. An additional year would give most of these students the opportunity to achieve the social and linguistic readiness base they need to find success in learning to read. For the disadvantaged students, the additional time would be well-used in acculturating and in gaining language experiences needed for performing adequately in school.

A later start would prevent much of the failure which is at the heart of the difficulty of these students. A later start would at least insure a successful beginning. Some would suggest that an earlier start is needed. This is nonsense. These children have been started too soon and failure is the consequence. There is no evidence to suggest that even the most able students are disadvantaged in any way by a more relaxed approach to beginning reading.

The cognitive, linguistic, and social readiness of most children simply emerge given a reasonable environment. These are not part of the typical curriculum. There are, however, readiness skills that are directly related to the printed language that must be learned. They should be part of a reading-readiness curriculum. These curricular items include basic concepts about print. They have to do with how the printed form of language represents the familiar spoken form.

Children need to be able to relate the familiar spoken form of language to print. This is not as easy for some children as it sounds. The format of spoken language is temporal, while the format of the printed form is visual. By temporal, I mean that the language appears in a time flow. A word is spoken and then is gone. Then appears the next and the next, etc. The flow of speech is such that there are no discernible spaces between most words. Speech is pretty much a continuous flow of sound. In print, however, masses of discourse appear all at once on the page. The temporal flow of speech must be related to the left-to-right, top-to-bottom sequence of print. Though speech has hardly any word boundaries, uniform spaces appear between words in print. Sentences have boundary markers and wider spaces.

Low achieving and disadvantaged children will not have any concepts about print. The notion of what a word is is abstract. You need this explicit knowledge in order to learn to read.

Many children who have had experience with books at home will already have developed these concepts about print before they start school. Sitting on a parent's lap and following a story's progress and watching the reader's actions gradually imparts this information.

All children need these concepts. If they haven't had previous experience with print, it will have to be part of the readiness activities. Before any reading instruction, children need to learn how the spoken format relates to the printed format.

The concept of word is very important. Without necessarily knowing what any words are, a student needs to understand the print conventions that isolate words. It may be difficult to consciously separate the continuous flow of sound into words. The simplest place to start is with the student's own name. Of all the words he encounters, this one will most likely be experienced as distinct and isolatable. Its printed form will relate easily to the spoken form. Other familiar names can follow. Trade names, especially fast-food franchises, can lend themselves to this. A photo or picture of the actual sign may be necessary at first.

Captions on simple pictures in the room, labels on all common objects in the room, and picture dictionaries are helpful. Reading aloud to children from charts and experience charts is easy practice. The teacher points to each word as the word is said. The students can associate the individual sounds of the words with the printed forms and begin to discern the boundaries of words and their individual characteristics. The direction of the flow of print, left-to-right and top-to-bottom, is gradually learned through repetition of this concrete activity.

In preparing experience charts for students, the teacher writes each word letter-by-letter and says the words as they are printed. The distinct parts of the words, the letters, and their left-to-right order within words is noted. This is done each time an experience chart is prepared. Rereading of the charts further familiarizes the student with these important basic concepts about print.

Learning that letters make up words and learning the letter names are very helpful readiness skills. Letter recognition has long been recognized as an important reading-readiness skill. When students know the letters, their attention can be directed to words by the letters they begin or end with. Also, they can attend to words that share similar features. It is also helpful when teaching letter-to-sound associations. Words that begin or end with the same letters often begin or end with the same sound.

There need be no distinct transition between reading-readiness activities and reading instruction. Low achieving students benefit from a gradual transition that is governed by the rate of their own emerging skill.

When are students ready to begin reading? When they have learned the basic concepts about print and when they have sufficient receptive language maturity to comprehend the material, they will read if it is read aloud to them. When students can point to individual words and identify words that begin with the same letters, they demonstrate mastery of basic concepts about print. When they can answer questions that summarize the content of a reading selection, they have enough language ability to learn to read that selection.

The big difference that separates low achieving students from their higher achieving peers concerns how long it will take to learn to read that selection. If both groups of students are ready to learn to read, it will take about 15 to 20 percent more time for the low achieving student to learn to read the selection (Hargis et al., 1988; Gates, 1930). Unfortunately, the lock-step movement does not permit this added time. All students are required to move on to the next page, selection, unit, or grade in unison.

The amount of time needed by low achieving students is directly related to the additional repetition they need to learn to recognize words. Word recognition must be distinguished from word identification (Hargis, 1982). Word recognition is what occurs when a word is sufficiently familiar to be recognized instantly. Word identification is what is done to call to mind the familiar spoken counterpart of a word that is still unfamiliar in its printed form. Words can be identified by several processes. The most direct approach is to have a tutor or teacher tell the student what the word is, or the student can use word-identification skills, such as context, or letter-sound associations to figure out what the word is.

Words must be successfully identified a sufficient number of times in order to become familiar enough to be recognized instantly. Repetition is the important factor in learning to recognize words. The amount of repetition needed to learn to recognize words is not often appreciated. The reason seems to be that we are concerned with various so-called methods of teaching word identification more than a mundane issue such as repetition. It is, however, repetition that is fundamentally important in learning to recognize words. Gates (1930) found that the average first grader needs about 35 repetitions of a word before he learns to recognize it instantly.

Gates systematically controlled the introduction and repetition rates for students in three first grade classrooms for the school year. He found that there was a range of repetition needs. The more able students required an average of only twenty repetitions, while the slowest group needed an average of fifty-five.

The repetition was provided in context in the reading material given to the students. Word recognition was checked in isolation. The words were tested on lists. Subsequent research (Hargis et al, 1988) confirms Gates's findings. Additionally, the amount of repetition low achieving students need when the words were presented in isolation was studied. It was found that on average, words need about 12 percent more repetition if they are presented to the student in isolated drill activities. Flash card presentation was used in this portion of the study.

Repetition is required until words are recognized instantly. Systems of word identification are needed for unfamiliar words until they are learned. Remember, repetitions are not effective unless students identify the word each time it is repeated. Simply presenting a word to a student a specified number of times will be ineffective unless the student also identifies it each time. The conscious association between printed word and spoken word must be made in order for the repetition to be a true one.

Provisions for identification are needed to produce true repetitions. These repetitions can be supported or independent identification processes. Teachers, tutors, peer tutors, or cooperative team members can simply tell a student each word that he can't independently identify. Choral reading, reading, and listening to tape-recorded passages simultaneously provides supported identification.

Independent repetition processes most often involve decoding, that is, using letter-sound associations, or phonics. Also, the use of context, or context together with phonics, may be used to identify words.

There are limitations to the use of independent identification activities at the beginning levels. First of all, the beginning reader will have learned relatively few identification skills. Further, a large percentage of the most commonly occurring words are not decodable, or readily so. The beginner's stock of known words will be small and context, by definition, must be made of known words. Therefore, the independent use of context will necessarily be limited. So, the beginner needs lots of supported repetition to build a good stock of known printed words and to build some confidence and feel success at actual reading.

The typical basal reading program does not provide for the repetition needed by low achieving students (Hargis 1985, 1987). The number of times the words are repeated in basal texts is inconsistent and almost never reaches adequacy for low achieving students. Remember, this is simply the number of times the words are repeated in textual material, and this in no way assures that the words are identifiable and are real repetitions of the words.

For low achieving students, the burden of unknown words increases in the reading materials they are moving through. The repetition, for them, is inadequate, so the words that make up the basal vocabularies remain largely unknown and increasingly formidable as the number of different words increases. The Matthew effects begin working with grim results.

Teachers assume that the method of teaching word identification is inappropriate for these students. They may change basal series or they may add on a supplemental word identification skill program. Neither of these are of benefit to the student. What they need is adequate supported repetition of words. Teaching word-identification skills to these students, with the hope that they will be applied to the now huge number of unknown words that face them at every turn, is a hope that is not to be fulfilled.

Independent word-identification skills can be used successfully if the reading material given the student is at an instructional reading level. In other words, if the number of new words a student must figure out in a reading selection doesn't exceed about 4 percent, the student will likely be able to use word-identification skills independently. The new words will appear among known words which provide the contextual support needed for their ready identification. Coupling the use of context with other decoding skills makes possible independent word identification. If the number of unknown words exceeds 4 percent, comprehension falls off rapidly (Betts, 1946). The loss of comprehension is the demonstration of the loss of the use of context. The use of context requires meaning. Unfamiliar words are predicted by what they are likely to be, given the meaning of the surrounding discourse. If the percentage of unknown words increases, comprehension diminishes, helpful context is lost, and a student is left with only whatever phonics skill he has acquired to figure out a too large burden of unknown words.

Remember, at the instructional level, only as many as one in twenty words can be unknown. This is a challenging level of difficulty. It is not possible for students to get good repetition from frustration level reading material independently. To use material of such difficulty with a student, word identification must be supported. Someone will have to work with the student to help him or tell him what many of the unknown words are.

Supported word identification is often labor-intensive. It requires a teacher or tutor to be with the student while using the material. Students need the opportunity to read independently and practice independent word identification. Students need some instructional level reading material. Further, they need material that is even easier, material that is at the independent reading level. At this level, they encounter fewer than 2 percent unknown words. They can read without concerns of word identification. They can enjoy and learn to enjoy reading. Students gain in efficiency and fluency if they are given the opportunity to read at the independent level.

Whether supported or independent, students need to identify words until they can recognize them instantly. There is no shortcut to improving reading skill.

We have the mistaken view that the method of teaching word identification is the principle factor involved when a student is not learning to read. Teachers will add supplemental word-identification programs or even change basal reader series in the hope that the different method of teaching decoding skills will improve a student's reading performance. This is done despite the obvious fact that the student was not able to benefit from the repetition provided in the material first used. The student was at a frustration level of difficulty in all reading activities. Changing methods has no effect unless the vehicle for providing the word repetition is also changed. Either the student needs supported word identification with the materials or he needs materials that are at an instructional level of difficulty that permit him to pursue word identification independently.

As was emphasized earlier, we do not seem to appreciate the amount of repetition low achieving students need in learning to read. This need is greater than is provided for in current reading curricula and materials. Teachers will have to provide for it if the students are going to make reasonable progress. The optimistic side of the issue of repetition is that the need declines as reading skill increases. Our data show that the need declines by half from the first to the third grade level. Stated another way, a student who requires about 50 repetitions of a word when he starts learning to read will only require about 25 repetitions by the time he acquires third grade reading skill. As reading becomes a natural, receptive language process, there is evidence that learning to recognize new words takes only a few trials. I have even observed, in very proficient readers, what seems to be one-trial learning of new words.

Commercially prepared, basal reading programs do not match the readiness needs and the repetition needs of low achieving or disadvantaged students.

So, how should beginning reading proceed with these students? I prefer the language experience approach for several reasons: It makes for an uninterrupted transition from readiness to reading. The language used in the reading material is drawn from the students themselves and, therefore, is assuredly familiar to them. The experience base necessary to comprehend the selection is also guaranteed, since the students were participants in the experience summarized in print. The latter two points are especially important for disadvantaged students. This approach also encourages the integration of other language arts activities with it. Finally, it encourages much repetition through rereading and copying activities.

Word identification is not a particular problem with the language experience approach. The students made the association between familiar spoken words with their printed form as each word was written on the experience chart. Rereading each story is done with little support in word identification.

As the students begin reading from books, one standard practice should be avoided. This is "at sight" oral reading. A teacher or peer should read the selection or story to the student before the student required to read it. This makes all of the words in the story far more predictable. The word-identification burden is considerably reduced, and the students are often able to read materials that would otherwise be too difficult. As the student reads the selection, peer tutors, fellow team members, or the teacher should provide immediately any assistance with word identification a student wants or needs. The student should reread the selection until all the words are familiar, and he can read the selection as an introduction to another student. These selections should be very short initially, not longer than can be read in a minute or two.

When students begin reading independently, it is important that they be given materials and books that they can read successfully. The language should be as predictable and familiar as possible, and foremost, it should be at the students' individual instructional or independent reading level. The best way to facilitate the development of independent word-identification skills is to provide students with reading material in which they are able to apply, and therefore practice, independent word identification. This is instructional level reading material.

Word-identification skill activities should not be separated from actual reading as they so often are in commercial programs. These skills are often relegated to follow-up activities in workbooks and on worksheets. They should be a part of introducing a real reading activity, used while reading the selection, and then a part of the comprehension check which follows. This procedure was called the intrinsic method by Arthur Gates (1930).

When word-identification skill practice is separated from real reading, it will not become a usable skill. Transfer of training will not occur. The teaching and application of these skills should be a part of reading activities. Practice in actually using the skills is fundamental to really learning them.

Keep in mind, however, that the most important part of learning to recognize words is repetition. Don't let an emphasis on subskill teaching divert time that would better be used at actual reading activities. Activities in which the student is getting this necessary repetition are leading to both an increase in word-recognition skill and word-identification skill.

Writing

Writing has reading as a readiness base, but it requires additional different cognitive skills. Both reading and writing are graphic, but reading is receptive, and writing is expressive.

Earlier, reading was likened to following the guidance of a map while writing was likened to the preparation of a coherent map. The ability to prepare a followable map requires some familiarity with maps, and writing requires the same kind of familiarity with print. When one reads, one is following the mental map provided by the writer. When one writes, one is preparing such a map. Writing is complex. There are many levels of written expression. These levels range from literature and technical writing to daily, routine writing of lists, messages, directions, notes, and letters. Some deal with pleasure and aesthetics, some with vocational and independent living skill.

The upper levels can emerge if there is talent for linguistic expression. That level is not a consideration here. The acquisition of the more functional skill is.

Written language contains the skills of handwriting and spelling. It also requires some skill at punctuation. Handwriting is a finite, concrete task and is readily learnable over the primary grades. Spelling is a task of greater scale than handwriting. Spelling curricula are more varied, have different subskill emphases, different objectives, and even present different word lists. Punctuation skill is by far the most difficult to learn. Sentence punctuation is more than knowing what an uppercase letter and a period is. A student must acquire explicit knowledge of what a sentence is. Additional punctuation requires explicit knowledge of still more difficult areas of sentence grammar. There is a great deal of variety in the ways punctuation is taught.

When handwriting is legible, words spelled well enough to be decodable, and sentences formed sufficiently well to be intelligible, some compositional skill must be learned. Certainly enough compositional skill must be learned to organize sentences into simple sets of directions, or to summarize events to enclose in a friendly letter or a legal statement. Methods of teaching composition are quite varied. Here, again, little agreement exists on how it should be taught. One thing is certain though; the typical methods used frustrate and demoralize most low achieving students.

How can written language be presented to low achieving and disadvantaged students so that they can succeed and progress? There are so many methods to choose from we often just try another if students are failing. Regardless of what methods are used, the amount of failure remains the same. The basic problem precluding the success and progress of low achieving students is that these various methods of teaching the components of written language are presented in lock-step without regard to the instructional level needs of low achieving students.

The first and most obvious component of writing is the handwriting itself. Handwriting must become at least legible enough not to interfere with getting the message. So, handwriting is only the vehicle for presenting the message. It is a tool skill that needs to be developed early. It needs to be used efficiently, so the skill must be internalized and automatic. It must be learned so that it can be used without conscious effort.

Handwriting cannot be judged in the same way that other curricular areas are. It cannot be judged right or wrong like a multiplication fact or a spelling word. It is compared to a standard. How close it comes to the standard determines the grade. I believe in being very flexible in judging against any standard other than legibility. Everyone develops a distinctive handwriting style very early, so deviations must be acceptable.

It is also not a good idea to compare a student's performance by using group standards. Students should not be judged by what others are producing. They should be judged based on what they are producing. There will be a range of developmental differences and ability levels in any classroom. In regard to handwriting, a student should be permitted to perform as well as he can and have that performance honored. The student should then be given only that amount of work that he can do with accuracy and success. If a student's performance is judged unacceptable, it is quite likely that he is being given a task that is too difficult. Poor handwriting may actually be produced by giving a student drill work at which he cannot achieve a high degree of legibility. He is, in effect, practicing illegibility.

The standard for the instructional level in handwriting activities is basically the same as for other drills. A student should be given no more work than he can practice with 95 percent legibility. For example, if a student is practicing forming isolated letters, he should be given no more different letters to practice than can be formed with 95 percent legibility.

Since legibility is the objective, legibility should be practiced. This instructional level is designed to insure success and legibility. The number of different letters that can be practiced with high legibility will vary, but the performance standard should remain the same.

In the typical classroom, all the students are given the same worksheet or drill activity. This will produce variable performance, and for those few students for whom the task is too difficult, the activity will be negative. These students will not perform up to classroom standards. They will both fail and practice illegibility.

There are few commercial handwriting programs. There are, however, many different spelling programs. Consequently, when a student is found to be a poor speller, a different spelling program is likely to be selected for him. The principle problem, however, is not to be found in the spelling program. The problem is the mismatch between the student's skill level and the level of difficulty of the spelling instruction. The solution to the problem is again making this match.

All programs have normative standards. When applied to students at the low end of the spelling ability range, they cause failure. Any of the spelling programs, when applied with these standards, will cause about the same amount of failure and in the same students. The solution becomes one of selecting individual instructional level standards.

Groups of students are given a twenty-word spelling list at the beginning of the week. They practice during the week and on Friday they take a test. Performance will vary. The point is that performance should not vary. Each student should be given no more words on Monday than he can learn to spell correctly by Friday.

A question arises here. How will he learn to spell well if you reduce the number of words? The answer is, of course, that he will at least be learning to spell as many words as he can. Missed words are evidence of words not learned and practice time wasted. Part of the solution to teaching spelling to these students is to give only the number of words to practice that they can learn successfully.

Ultimately, most skill at spelling is acquired through writing and reading. It is important that students do as much of these activities as possible and be successful at them as well. Students should never feel fear or apprehension about writing. Papers that return covered with red marks and negative comments lead to students becoming so fearful of making errors that they avoid writing, or write only in the sparest, most minimal forms and amounts, that reduces the likelihood of getting the dreaded red marks and corrections.

Students should always feel absolutely free to express themselves in writing without fear of making errors. Spelling errors in written expression provide an opportunity for corrective feedback. The feedback should not be in the form of a red mark or grade. Writing should be edited, not graded. Feedback should be for purposes of editing. It should occur as soon as possible, and it should be done with the notion that writing is not really completed until it has been edited.

Cooperative teams can be very helpful in this editing process. Team members should provide as much feedback as possible at the first stage. Then the teacher can provide the final suggestions. All students will produce acceptable papers at the end. Some may take longer, but the end must be the same. The feedback and correction that occurs at each stage constitutes additional repetition and drill leading to fluency and achievement in handwriting, spelling, and composition. The practice being gained is the most meaningful and utilitarian. The words being learned are not from isolated, frequently non-meaningful, word lists. The words written are those intended by the student. The most common, most important spelling words get more practice.

These writing activities should occur regardless of the spelling program in use. These writing activities should also occur regardless of the language arts program in use. Composition skill is improved by actually composing. Students need much opportunity to write if composition skills are to improve. The editing and repeated drafting provide good repetition.

It is important to remember this point about a student's writing ability. A student's instructional level in writing is whatever he is able to produce at that moment! What is produced should not be held up to normative standards. A student's current writing should be the starting place. The problems it has which most interfere with intelligibility should be the priority for instruction and editing.

Writing should not be a painful activity. Students should not be rewarded with red marks when they attempt to spell a new word. Any unambiguous spelling approximation should be considered a triumph. Any attempt at all should be honored. These students need success, and the practice necessary for achievement only occurs with success. Success at written composition depends on the teacher's willingness to accept whatever a student is currently producing as his instructional level.

Chapter 16

ARITHMETIC

Arithmetic would seem to be a straightforward, concrete subject, but it is not. Several very different philosophic influences have dictated approaches to arithmetic curriculum construction. These views on curriculum construction inevitably interact with learning problems and perspectives on teaching and learning. The first part of this chapter attempts to sort these issues out so that the readers can see where they are in regard to arithmetic curriculum and instruction and see what the contending issues are. Next, my philosophic view on arithmetic curriculum and instruction for low achieving and disadvantaged students is described.

Arithmetic skills learned in school but not used later may be lost. This problem brings up the issue of relevance in arithmetic curricula. Three perspectives on curriculum construction influence relevance for low achieving students. These are: the basic skills position, the understanding or new math position, and the social utility or life skill position. Though not necessarily absent in the first two, only the latter position takes a direct stand on relevance. The relative influence of each of these curricular influences is not static but changes with the prevailing mood.

Two of these positions appear to be in opposition. The skill versus understanding debate has been going on since early in this century. Those who emphasize computational algorithms and problem-solving skills are on one side and those who emphasize "understanding" and "meaningful" instruction on the other. This latter group currently is associated with the "new math" and is most associated with the period from the late 1950s to the late 1970s. The former group seems to be spearheaded by a "back-to-basics" movement. These curricula can, and often do, become ends in themselves without sufficient regard to their real-world application for low achieving and disadvantaged students.

Preceding the skill-versus-understanding controversy by many years, and lurking in the background throughout the above-mentioned debate, has been the notion of social utility. It goes under a variety of titles, including *consumer math, life math, practical math,* and even *survival math.* Its head emerges as a result of testing or observation of the fact that some students can't handle day-to-day math problems such as making change, balancing a checkbook, or figuring sales tax even after completing one or the other curriculum. Advocates of "practical" math have been around since Ben Franklin used the notion to promote the inclusion of arithmetic in the curriculum.

Here then is the issue of relevance. The new math curriculum seems more concerned with students who are academically talented and interested in math as a subject. The basic skills approach concerns itself with simple mastery and accuracy in computation as the end objectives. Neither approach seems to recognize that the math related to life situations poses considerable challenge to low achieving and disadvantaged students and requires direct, thoughtful curricular emphasis. Most of these students need a much greater social utility emphasis.

There are a number of issues in elementary arithmetic instruction that are important but generally unresolved. This is true, particularly in regard to the education of the low achieving learner. I will attempt to delineate these issues with sufficient detail so that their relevance to the education of these children will be more apparent and that these notions can be integrated into a more useful perspective on arithmetic curriculum. The first issue is meaningfulness. The problem of making mathematics learning meaningful has been a consideration of educators for many years. Resnik and Ford (1981) have a thoughtful review of meaningfulness in mathematics instruction. On the surface, this important idea, meaningfulness, may seem rather simple. However, two quite different approaches have emerged. Very early, the drill and practice of unrelated procedures and facts isolated from application was criticized. Efforts were made to relate each fact and procedure to practical activities where they are needed in dealing with problems in daily living, i.e. making change, measuring a room for carpeting, calculating wages, etc. In this way use and meaning were equated. This seems to have been a rational, practical notion.

The end of the 1950s brought together a number of forces which were to affect the course of math curriculum development. Two very influential conferences were held concerning the nature of math instruction. The first was in 1959 at Woods Hole, Massachusetts which included educators, psychologists, mathematicians, and scientists. The other conference, which involved primarily mathematicians, was held in 1963 in Cambridge, Massachusetts. At this conference, proposals were made for curriculum change that had many dramatic effects. From these conferences a very different approach to meaningfulness emerged. Now meaningful learning meant linking underlying structure and concept with the mathematical fact or procedure being learned. This approach is an intellectual one in which meaning is related to knowledge of the structure underlying the fact or process rather than meaning being related to a use of the fact or process. They proposed a conceptual rather than a computational approach to mathematics instruction (Resnick and Ford, 1981). Meaningfulness would depend not on the relevance of computation in real-life tasks but on the extent to which it related to the structure of mathematics as a subject in and of itself.

Another way that meaningfulness can be viewed is quite apart from the two views just discussed. This view has to do with concreteness, which can be seen in the following example presenting the concept of *place value*. A concrete set of objects that can be manipulated might be used to find answers and formulate concepts in regard to place value. These objects may be any common, convenient-to-manipulate items such as straws, blocks, chips, marbles, etc. The number 76 would be represented by seven sets or stacks of ten chips and one of six. In other words, seven tens plus the six. The students would be directed to the standard notation for the number that this concrete array represents. This concrete procedure is used to assist in teaching an abstract construct which concerns the number system.

The notion of place value, per se, is not necessary in learning a number. It is also very reasonable to learn to regroup ("carry" or "borrow") without being introduced to place-value. Place-value, however, has much to do with understanding or the meaning of mathematical structures. Yet, it is actually more abstract than counting or addition and subtraction with carrying and borrowing which are the very things it is supposed to make more meaningful. From my vantage point, it is far easier for low achieving students to learn place value well after some of the basic computational skills have been mastered.

Concreteness can and has been used in teaching simple facts and computation directly. Concrete objects can be counted or manipulated as needed to solve immediate problems without ever stopping to deal with concepts or underlying mathematical structures. This is a step closer to reality and is a more sensible approach for these students. Counting and computation can be achieved more expeditiously with this direct, concrete approach.

In some computational activities, such as extracting a square root, it is difficult to effectively use concreteness as a learning facilitator. Here, for many children, there may be no meaningful purpose to be found for its application in reality, thus making its mastery much less likely. As curriculum items become increasingly abstract or less common in the day-to-day world, concreteness will be less available for use in teaching to an increasingly larger group of children, and the need to teach such must be seriously questioned.

In my view, meaningfulness in terms of the structure of mathematics is an interesting curricular area, but it is misplaced when applied to low achieving and disadvantaged learners. When it is more difficult that the thing it is being used to explain, certainly it loses its value. Mathematicians, interested in the study of mathematics, formulated and delineated these concepts, concepts that are independent of the practical computational aspects of mathematics and should be considered separately in the curriculum. Further, they are inappropriate for inclusion to any extent with low achieving students.

The term "rote learning" may imply learning without meaning to many. To some, the term "drill" can be use interchangeably. From my perspective, rote learning refers to the mode of presentation more than it does the drill required for mastery. For many low achieving students, rote associative learning is a strength to be capitalized on. In rote learning the procedures for computation are very simply and directly demonstrated to the student, and he is assisted in duplicating the process until it can be done with some independence. Understanding or meaningfulness of rules is not an issue. Concreteness is not necessarily a constituent of this introduction process. This is not to say that it wouldn't have a facilitating effect on learning, but it is not per se a part of rote learning. There is no attempt to encourage the student to deduce or induce rules involved in the computation. It is not necessary for the process itself to be meaningful. Needless to say, rote teaching will most affect computation learning. Reasoning, unfortunately for many low achieving students, does not readily lend itself to rote teaching procedures. The area of reasoning (word or thought problems) requires generalization of these computation skills to varied individual problems which require different logical processes.

Discovery learning or methods of presentation can be considered the antithesis of rote procedures. As Resnik and Ford (1981) point out, "discovery learning" has often been proposed as the best approach to use in presenting new concepts in mathematics and other subject areas. Very generally, the discovery strategy is to make available all the relevant materials for a problem or a concept after which students are permitted to "browse" through the materials and test ideas until they discover relationships and rules on their own. A modification of "pure" discovery is called by some "guided" discovery. Learning in this procedure is fostered by guiding children through all the steps or conditions leading up to a conclusion but letting them come up with the actual rule themselves.

It should be pointed out that discovery learning is rather difficult to define precisely. Research in the area of discovery learning has been criticized because of the varied procedures used as discovery activities. Pure discovery procedures, however, seldom show advantage over guided discovery. In my research, only academically talented students used pure discovery without much disadvantage. The more rote methods were clearly superior for low achieving students.

Drill is an important part of math instruction. How much repetition or practice is required for mastery of a skill? Are there any considerations that affect the amount of repetition? What is mastery? What role does review play in learning?

When all the prerequisite skills have been learned, then drill can be effective in learning a new skill. Obviously, a student is not ready for a task if he does not have the prerequisite skills. Drill is not nearly as effective in remembering nonsense items as it is in learning concrete, meaningful ones. Math items for which prerequisite skills are missing become nonsense items.

Assuming a child has the prerequisite skills for learning a new item, how much drill will then be required? Resnik and Ford (1981) reviewed research related to the relative difficulty of arithmetic problems and the amount of drill they require for mastery. The early research did not attempt to find why problems were easier or harder. They simply ranked them by what seemed to be their ease or difficulty in learning or the number of trials to mastery. The relative difficulty is likely due, however, to the amount of mental processing involved in specific problems. Loftus and Suppes (1972) predicted problem difficulty by what they called "structural variables" which seem to contribute to their complexity.

The three determinants of the amount of drill required for learning are: readiness (having the prerequisite skills), the complexity of the computational activity, and the concreteness of its original presentation. Unfortunately, on an individual basis, it may take great effort to plan for teaching and drill using all three considerations. Improvement in computer-assisted drill offers promise in removing some drudgery in the preparation of drill activities.

Another consideration in regard to drill or practice is "spacing." It is generally known that spaced practice is more effective than massed practice for most arithmetic skills. In other words, practice sessions with limited amounts of repetition spaced over several days are more effective than the same amount of repetition concentrated in one period.

Isolated drill and mixed-drill activities may be considered at different stages of learning. Extended practice with similar types of problems is isolated drill. Interspersing various types with others represents mixed drill. It seems that generally the interspersed drill is more productive, but that isolated drill is best when a new item has first been presented and needs to be established. Also, isolated drill is a helpful remedial procedure in eliminating learned error patterns. Mixed drill is used for maintenance and mastery.

The ultimate function of drill is to increase fluency or rate of response as well as accuracy. The student who is fluent and accurate has reached the level of automatic response to the computational procedure. Ultimately, this will increase the efficiency in problem solving, because the student can handle many of the computational constituents of the problem automatically, thereby reducing the total memory load and time required to determine the answer.

What level of accuracy is the expected outcome of drill? For the basic facts 100 percent is desirable. However, 95 percent appears to be sufficient to demonstrate mastery in areas of simple computation. Lesser levels should be accepted in more complex algorithms where several computational procedures compound the likelihood of inadvertent error.

How much new information can be introduced at a given time? In Miller's (1956) classic article, memory limitations appear to hold this to about seven "pieces" plus or minus two. In introducing new items in arithmetic the issue is more complex than this relatively simple storage example. It comes fairly close, though, when relatively less complex items, such as counting and basic facts, are presented. This, of course, can be true only if the student is ready for the presentation of the new items. The important thing to remember here is that there are limitations on the amount of new information that can be introduced. Also, when planning drill activities, the relative newness of the item may add some memory burden. The fact that an item has been introduced previously and has been subject to some drill does not mean that it cannot contribute difficulty to retrieval from memory.

Practically speaking, students should be given no more new items than they can practice accurately. Remember, they must be practiced correctly to be learned. Certainly, if a student encounters so much unfamiliar material in drill activity that he can no longer stay engaged in it, it has too many unknown or unfamiliar items. When a student misses more than a quarter of the items in a drill activity, he will have difficulty staying on task, and he will have too much opportunity to practice errors.

Thought or word problems pose a different set of difficulties. Skill in computation will be a necessary, but insufficient base for dealing with the solution of word problems. Some problems are expressed in a single sentence. Frequently, however, the problem will have several sentences which take on the structure of a paragraph. The number of computational steps may be few or many. Sentence complexity can vary enormously. The more complex the sentence structure, the more difficult is the reading level. Complex sentences increase the logical processes required for problem solution.

Word problems very seldom state which computation activities should be used. A student is far more likely to see a word problem of the form (a) than (b): (a) If Joe is six feet tall and Fred is five feet tall, then how much shorter is Fred than Joe? (b) What number remains if you subtract five from six?

Word problems, requiring only very simple computational activities to solve, can be stated in very complex language that obscures which computation should be done. In word problems students need to identify a pattern or gain an insight from the language to find the correct computational process. Are skills in gaining these insights and seeing these patterns teachable? To a certain extent they are. However, the teaching must be systematic. The language complexity must be carefully controlled.

For some students transfer of these skills to situations that vary only slightly from the learned form will be quite difficult. How novel a new problem can be is a consideration that must be made anew for each student.

A great range of things can be taught to most children, regardless of the perspective of the curriculum from which they are drawn. A question that must be made here is: Is the expenditure of time and effort worth it? If the expenditure of time and effort is at the expense of teaching that helps students deal with persisting life problems, then the answer is no. Each curricular item should lead to the achievement of greater independence in dealing with life's problems. Stated in more practical terms, the curriculum should help insure that the low achieving student can remain healthy, out of jail, and employed. The reverse of these conditions unfortunately occurs in far greater percentages for these students than for their higher achieving peers.

Arithmetic curricula have tendencies toward effusiveness in regard to vocabulary and special mathematical terms. A great many of these terms have no utility beyond the classroom. When was the last time that you used the terms "minuend" or "subtrahend" with the clerk at a checkout counter? There are a multitude of excess terminologies that are used with computational activities. Other such terms include: integer, addend, multiplicand, quotient, rational and irrational (numbers), numerator, denominator, and disjoint, null, finite, universal (sets). There are terms for properties such as: distributive, associative, commutative, closure, etc. There are also a variety of symbols that can be troublesome. A rule of thumb is, if the average adult uses the arithmetic operation which includes such terms but does so without knowing what the terms are, then the value of such terms is trivial and quite possibly negative. The teaching of many of these terms, which are only replacements for common serviceable words likely known by students already, may be impediments to the acquisition of computational skills. In the end they need be presented only if they are part of some proficiency test.

Some arithmetic curricula appear to have little utility in the real world. There also seems to be considerable variation between the way arithmetic problems occur in reality and the way they are presented in the classroom. Transfer of training is not likely when there is such variation. One has only to read a grocery ad in the newspaper to see that layout and abbreviation used in the equations to calculate price per unit are quite different than the format for the same computations presented in class. The common commercial formats for consumer math activities should be related to computational format for the classroom.

The nature of word or thought problems should be carefully reviewed in regard to their utility. The variety and complexity of the logic involved, as well as the readability levels of such problems, needs to be placed in a much more manageable order.

If A trade a barrel of onions to B, worth 2 pence the bushel, in exchange for a sheep worth 4 pence and a dog worth a penny, and C kill the dog before delivery, because bitten by same, who mistook him for D, what sum is still due to A from B, and which party pays for dog, C or D, and who gets the money? If A, is the penny sufficient, or may he claim consequential damages in the form of additional money to represent the possible profit which might have incurred from the dog, and classifiable as earned increment, that is to say, usufruct?

This "word" problem was posed by the character, Hank Morgan, in *A Connecticut Yankee in King Arthur's Court* by Mark Twain. Most of the difficulties that have been associated with word problems are to be found in this comic piece. Arithmetic reasoning is most associated with the way a problem is expressed linguistically. This is apart from the "problem" solving required for working through algorithms already stated in the standard notations. When low achieving students are introduced to word problems, every effort should be made to state the problem directly and concretely. The problems ultimately dealt with should represent utilitarian life problems as closely as possible.

Morgan's problem illustrates well that short-term memory is quickly burdened by the number of steps involved as well as the distractors that are included. If the problem's constituents are physically or graphically present, it will aid considerably in its solution. This should be a necessary context when word problems are initially presented.

Verbal problem-solving ability will necessarily be limited by the skill a student has in doing the computation required. However, the logical and memory load make problems difficult much beyond their actual computational demands. Skill with all the computational constituents of the problem is a necessary, but by no means sufficient, skill base for doing verbal reasoning problems.

Complexity of verbal problems can be very much likened to readability. If the passage is comprehensible or within the readability level of a student, he or she is probably capable of doing it. Certainly, if the problem is in print, inability to read and comprehend the problem will be the foremost difficulty.

Chapter 17

CURRICULUM CONTENT

The three R's are the curricular areas that dominate most of the attention given low achieving and disadvantaged students. They are important in other areas as well; they are tool skills used in most other subject areas. This is particularly true of reading, and its importance is an accepted fact. Writing and arithmetic are viewed as extremely important, if only somewhat less so than reading. These three were discussed in the previous two chapters. The other content subjects that make up the curriculum are subject to more controversy.

There are some broad subject areas that are included in most curricula. In their general sense, they are not controversial. Everyone agrees that science, social studies, literature, and even vocational and physical education are important. However, the particulars of each content area are varied and subject to much criticism and controversy.

Criticism comes from various religious and political groups. It comes from non-partisan, well-meaning critics who simply want all students to do better, score higher, achieve more. This latter group usually advocates more rigor in the curriculum. Their solution to poor achievement is to require more of the students. This means requiring more math, science, history, and more homework. These efforts, though well-meaning, are devastating for low achieving and disadvantaged students.

We have developed an idealized image of what students should achieve. It is a scholarly image. It is certainly an appropriate objective for a good many students, but we can't expect it of all students. We must have a more reasonable utilitarian image and objective for low achieving students or they will achieve nothing positive at all. The source of their problem is one of forcing them to fit curricular structures that are too demanding for them.

Recently, a model high school with a model curriculum was described. Naturally, its curriculum was full of rigor, much math, science, great literature, and history. It would be an excellent school for those students who would be able to benefit from such a course of study. However, we cannot make low achieving students scholars simply by forcing them into such a course of study. The proposed school is called James Madison High; it would be a deadly place for low achieving and disadvantaged students. We must learn to consider a student's individual ability level, and we must learn to honor achievement to potential as much as achievement to the standard of a curriculum — even one as lofty as that posed for James Madison High School. We must structure success into the very core of the curriculum and methods. We cannot do this if we require the same thing for all students.

Not all students are, or should be, college-bound, and not nearly as many students should be failing and dropping out of school. Schools need to attend to more basic objectives. They need to keep students who are failing and dropping out in school. They need to help students who are underachieving to achieve to their potential. This means that we must permit students to work at many different levels of curricular difficulty. It also means that we must change the content of some courses and curricula to permit students to function as citizens.

We need to consider curricular adjustments that help students to stay healthy, out of jail, and employed. Our current lack of curricular attention to these needs permits low achieving students to become societal burdens.

Let me describe another idealized high school, one that respects individual differences, structures success, and honors modest attainments such as being able to live independently without being a burden on society. Let me call it the Emiliano Zapata High School. It has baseline objectives for all students. The curriculum which leads to these objectives is called the healthy, out-of-jail, and employed curriculum, the HOJE curriculum.

A different perspective on curriculum is used in Zapata than in Madison. At Madison, the curriculum objectives are set above the basal level for many students. It is a curriculum that is held above the reach of students. It is felt that students must reach up, be challenged, to achieve these lofty academic objectives. Only in the reaching can they be attained. You must have very high expectations for all students. Slow students must be challenged.

At Zapata High, the curriculum recognizes that success is fundamental to achievement; that challenge means a double standard will be applied. It honors the basic life skills that make a student an independent citizen. The curriculum must have these as the basal objectives in order that low achievers can succeed as well as their counterparts at the upper end of the academic curriculum. However, the Zapata High curriculum is not just HOJE; that is just the minimum, the basal expectation for all students. If HOJE objectives are all that a particular low achiever can attain, well, that is fine and it is a superb, honorable accomplishment. However, it is only the basal objective. All students who have the ability and talent will work toward the same academic goals that the Madison High students do. The difference between the two schools is that at Zapata individual differences and students can work along a curriculum ladder at a pace that permits success. It expects different students to come out with many different skills or academic knowledge levels. It expects, however, at least the HOJE skills to be mastered.

The Madison school has only the top academic objectives to work toward. It will produce many casualties. The top academic students will survive. The low achievers will drop out or come out with no independent living skills at all.

Discounting a life skill orientation to the curriculum, just the attainment of a diploma has utility in and of itself. Also, even if the curriculum remains academic rather than life-skill-oriented, it should be paced to individual student needs. Failure is non-productive. The students will not be able to achieve to their potential or attain a diploma. Success must dominate the curricular assignment to low achieving students. Students must be placed at a level on the curricular continuum, whichever curriculum it is, where they can experience success. They must be placed at their appropriate instructional level.

Zapata High has a flexible curriculum. Students can emphasize a life-skill curriculum or an academic curriculum. The curriculum may be a balance of the two, depending on the students' needs. The balance may tip more or less in either direction, again depending on the individual. Moreover, life skills will be integrated in academic subjects wherever possible and appropriate academic subjects will be integrated in the life skills. The curriculum will be assigned and structured to fit students. It will not be assigned to grades and courses.

Teachers at Zapata High are prepared to teach a heterogenous group of students. All of the teachers can teach any of the basic academic subject areas in addition to a specialty where they may be a resource person. This permits the merging of three curricular areas in most course work. These are the HOJE curriculum, the minimum competency or proficiency test curriculum, and the pre-college curriculum.

Course work is not tightly compartmentalized as it is in James Madison High, or for that matter in any conventional curriculum. All teachers feel an obligation to attend to all the curricular areas. That includes all levels of difficulty in each area. They all know that they must work with each student at whatever level he has attained when he arrives at their room.

Determining where instruction should start in any of the subject areas is a primarily important activity. A student's current instructional level in regard to the readiness requirements of the subject must be determined for each student. The scope and sequence of skills making up each curricular area should be used as a gauge or checklist to determine with precision where a student is. This is the student's entry or readiness level.

Readiness is determined by several factors. The present amount of progress along the sequence of subskills that makes up the curriculum is one. Having tool skills such as sufficient reading skill to use references and texts is another. Having sufficient maturity or experience to cope with the learning activity is still another.

Lack of maturity or experience can manifest itself in difficulty with most subject areas. Lack of experience may simply give the appearance of ignorance, but the areas of ignorance turn out to be skills prerequisite to the curricular topic at hand. For example, many intermediate grade students are not aware of the name of the county they live in or that they even live in something called a county. Many of the same students will not know the name of even one adjoining state. Yet, these notions are fundamental to understanding topics in social studies. Lack of experience frequently affects a student's vocabulary development. New words are learned as a student's range of experience increases. Every unfamiliar word is an additional obstacle to readability, and it represents a missing concept in whatever subject that it appears in. Disadvantaged students are particularly burdened by lack of common experience.

When a student lacks prerequisite skills, for whatever reason, instruction lacks meaningfulness and will be virtually impossible to benefit from. Meaningfulness is rooted in experience. Some experience must be direct; some can be provided through explanation and analogy. Experiences make learning any curricular item possible. Experiences are the concrete context that are necessary for much learning. Either the experience is provided in laboratory work, field trips, etc., or the instruction is related to pre-existing experience. Students need to have some concrete experience with space and directions before they can understand maps. Some things are not directly experienced but must be represented through models. Abstraction increases, but instruction is built on some form of previous experience.

Meaningfulness enhances learnability. The amount and nature of the experiences that are necessary to teach individual children varies. Meaningfulness and repetition are necessary to learning. Both of these are needed in greater measure with low achieving students.

The added need for experience and meaningfulness, together with the seldom-appreciated need for repetition, have a pronounced effect on the Zapata curriculum. Since the added experiences and repetition needed permit many fewer curricular items to be learned, there is constant careful curricular review to determine what are the most fundamentally important things to include.

When all of the constituents of typical curricula are presented, there are relatively few students who are sufficiently ready and able to learn them all. Low achieving and disadvantaged students will be bombarded with new items and facts, some of which they lack the experience to understand and few of which will be learned or remembered because their presentation is so fleeting.

American education brings much criticism down on itself, because so few students seem to know basic facts about history, government, economics, and science. However, I can assure you that legions of facts on these subjects are in public school curricula and are presented. This is precisely the problem. Too much is presented! So much is presented that the opportunity for learning so many different things is severely limited. The students' memories are overburdened with so many items that there is little possibility that even the more able students can store all this information for more than the short term long enough to pass a test. Too many or too much is introduced which in turn preempts the time needed for the prerequisite experiences, drill, and repetition of each so that it can be truly learned.

This formidable body of facts is laid out in the lock-step pattern through which each student must march. This is often done without regard to the students' readiness, prior experience or their varied learning rates. They are overwhelmed with information, much of which they cannot really learn.

The problem with the curriculum is not that it contains too little. It is that it contains far too much. And we are constantly tempted to add more and more.

At Zapata High, students are presented the maximum amount that they can learn. This means, however, that many fewer things can be presented. This also means that what is presented must be of high priority. The priority considerations have been discussed earlier. The most fundamentally important are the HOJE curriculum items. Other items are added to this, but still it depends on the individual student. No more new curricular items are added than a student is ready for or than he can master.

The net effect of this process is that the students are often presented much less, but they learn far more.

The reaction to this idea may be that this is all well and good, but how can this be managed in a subject such as literature? The fact is that standard literature anthologies usually pose reading difficulties far beyond the capabilities of low achieving and disadvantaged students. Readability is a primary consideration. No students will ever learn to enjoy or appreciate literature if their exposure to it comes without success and enjoyment from the beginning. This means finding material that is readable and appealing in content but still literature.

Requiring a student with a seventh grade reading level to read Julius Ceaser and memorize passages from it will almost assure that the student will hate it. No appreciation for literature or enjoyment of it comes from forcing students into books that they have neither the reading skill nor the background experiences to understand.

Anthologies should be constructed and specific reading selections should be made based on readability. Work of literary quality varies greatly in reading difficulty. The readability level of the material should be matched to the reading capability of individual students. At intermediate and secondary reading levels, readability formulas can do a fair job of estimating the difficulty of materials to use with low achieving students. Below third grade reading level, however, these formulas are too imprecise to make an accurate match without also checking a student's ability to read directly from the material. The student should be able to read the material at least at the instructional level.

Does the literature relate to the students' experience? Literature is certainly one way to broaden a student's knowledge of people and places outside his direct experience. However, it is helpful, and sometimes necessary, to select material that has content that is basically familiar to a student. It is also beneficial for the selections to have characters with whom these students can identify.

Enjoyment of reading and literature only comes when a student can understand it. This experience and opportunity is completely missing from the standard treatment of literature for low achieving and disadvantaged students.

I don't mean that "great" works should be abridged and watered down so that they can be understood. I believe that the objective of literature in the curriculum should be followed in spirit and to the letter. This means, however, that readable, relevant literature must be identified. Imposing standard lists and anthologies on these students meets neither the letter nor spirit of these objectives, and further, it makes these students hate the subject.

Social studies is a curricular area that is often crammed with details. The overwhelming numbers of names, dates, places, and events are neither meaningful, learnable or usable for low achieving students. This is not to say that there is not important social studies content for these students. There is important content on the social and legal structure of the community where the student must live and survive. Keeping on the right side of the law is often a matter of ignorance. The curriculum should be directed specifically to this issue.

Living peacefully and helpfully in social systems needs concrete attention. It takes long-term effort to learn that "one's freedom ends where one's neighbors's nose begins." Learning to be an acceptable, not an objectionable, citizen is a long-term effort. It is difficult to teach students not to drop trash wherever they happen to be if they are constantly surrounded by litter and the behavior that produces and encourages littering.

Geography must first be related to where the student is, no matter how restricted the experience. The instruction must be made meaningful. The students need to understand the area geography and transportation systems in sufficient detail to open employment opportunity that otherwise would simply be ignored.

How much history should be taught? Certainly, our history is important. Humans have abundant talent in repeating mistakes. Its importance notwithstanding, I cannot make a judgment on the specific, most important items of history that should be included. I will provide this fundamental guideline, however. Do not include any more than a given student can successfully learn. Overwhelming students with content will insure that they learn almost nothing.

How much science should be taught? The most important things have utility, and to be learned they must be meaningful. Science should be related to nutrition and health, safety, and problems of daily living. We live in a chemical, electronic, and mechanical environment of enormous complexity. The curriculum for low achieving students should first assist them in living safely and healthily within it.

How a student manages leisure-time activities is often critically important. If, with time on his hands, a student wanders through his neighborhood looking in windows, he will soon be in trouble. If there are many rather innocent ways of getting in trouble, there are many more that are not. Students must learn acceptable recreational activities that will fully engage their leisure time, not only while they are students but lifelong.

The portion of the curriculum that should be devoted to these problems is health, physical education and recreation. Less time here should be spent with conventional, competitive sports, and more time spent on individual activities that focus on fitness, health, and the use of leisure time. The activities learned should be available or easily performed in whatever the specific community has available. Jogging, hiking, or walking can be managed in some form almost everywhere. Organized fitness and athletic programs are more or less available everywhere. Special-interest clubs devoted to almost anything can be located. Bird-watching, woodworking, stamp collecting, coin collecting, and collecting and crafts of all sorts have devoted followers. Clubs devoted to automotive interests such as the Slant Six Club, the Datsun 510 Club, the Volkswagen Beetle Club, or the Corvair Club can engage the students and help them acquire and maintain affordable transportation. The social dimension of clubs and organizations is important and useful. The sense of community is maintained and the student is less likely to become isolated and enter a destructive activity or subculture.

Students need to learn to plan and engage their time fully. Organizing time around a part-time job can help the students learn work-related skills and prepare them for managing a second job which may be necessary for economic survival.

Vocational and career education needs to focus on survival or economic independence. Many vocational areas that have traditionally been emphasized in high schools are very technical and require abilities and talents that are not available in students any more than high academic talents are. At Zapata High the vocational training is geared to the ability levels of the students. Basic auto service such as tire repair and lubrication are included, since they are within the ability level of more of the students and they offer wider employment opportunity. Food service, janitorial work, yard work, and other basic services are also included. Community resources are used as the basic training centers wherever possible. Transfer and transition to work can be considered more effectively. Work study programs are emphasized.

Other technical training emphasizes basic household services, wiring, plumbing, and carpentry. These students, if they are to be independent, will have to handle much basic service themselves. They are unlikely ever to be able to afford having it done. Auto maintenance will be emphasized for those who must rely on cars for transportation. Transportation costs can be the largest portion of the budget. The emphasis is on operating and maintaining inexpensive cars safely.

Skill at how to improve one's standard of living while working at service economy wages are emphasized. These include skills at networking and trading. These also foster cooperation and a sense of community and community participation.

The Zapata High curriculum honors simpler things. Keeping healthy, out of jail and employed is an admirable attainment. The curriculum emphasizes things that make seemingly small accomplishments significant. It does everything it can to keep students off the streets, out of trouble and off drugs. By respecting these objectives and the students' need for success, the school shows the students respect. Show respect and get respect; Zapata high is respected by its students.

Chapter 18

HOMEWORK

Education reformers and critics almost always call for more homework. They have the misguided idea that if students simply spend more time trying to do schoolwork they will make great strides in achievement. The students apparently can't learn their lessons at school, so they must need more work at home.

The critics are correct in only one sense: time engaged in a learning activity is related to the amount learned. However, the deeper question is, can the students actually engage in doing the homework? After all, if the student can't do the work at school, how is he to do it at home? I am startled by the notion that many people actually think that students will somehow magically be able to do their work at home if they are having trouble doing it at school. And, if they can't do it at school, what they need is even more of it to do at home.

Indeed, more homework is viewed almost as a panacea. Far from being a panacea, homework, as it is currently prescribed, is downright poisonous to low achieving and disadvantaged students. When students are doing failing work in school, they will be doing failing work at home. If students can't do their homework correctly, several negative outcomes are likely.

The opportunity to practice errors is great. If the work is too difficult, the work that is done will be done incorrectly. In other instances, the work will not even be attempted because the student has no idea how to proceed with it. Homework that is too difficult is far worse than no homework at all.

Homework may require assistance from a family member in order to be done correctly. This may be an impossible demand on family resources. The help simply may not be there for a variety of reasons. Homework that requires assistance is not appropriate; this is work that should be done at school where the assistance can be planned.

Poor work habits result from inappropriate homework. Homework is unlikely to be done if students find that they can't do it satisfactorily or correctly. Students will learn to avoid doing homework when it can only be done unsatisfactorily when attempted. Students can only learn good work habits if they are given work that they can do.

The issue of homework permits teachers to shift the blame for lack of achievement to students and their families. If students aren't doing their homework, that means that it is the students' fault that they are not learning. Low achieving students just don't seem to do their homework. "I just can't make them do their homework" is an often-heard expression.

The students don't do their homework, so they get marked down even more. Their poor work in school is compounded by their inability to do their homework. The teachers judge that the problems with work at school are the result of the fact that the students are not doing the necessary follow-up work at home. There is certainly some truth in this for some students but not for most. Students who are able to do the homework can get necessary drill and practice at home. If they have family members that can help, they will get helpful corrective feedback. These students may fall behind if they don't do their homework. However, they are the students who are able to do their homework. The condition of these students may be erroneously generalized to low achieving students who can't do their homework.

For homework to be of benefit, it must be doable. Homework makes up much of the activities that follow introductory instruction. It must be clear that the student understood the initial instruction and that the homework activity is within the instructional level resources of each student. Remember that practice or drill is only real practice if the student gets it correct. If the student is given a reading assignment, the reading material must be at the student's instructional or independent reading level. Students can't get information from textual material that they can't read. If the work is drill for achieving fluency and mastery, it all should be already fairly familiar to the student. The student must be able to get all the elements of the practice correct, otherwise it doesn't lead directly to mastery or fluency. If the homework assignment includes reading to gain information on a subject, the books or selections used should be readable and the information extractable.

Homework should not be used in place of basic instruction. Do not expect homework to overcome deficiencies in instruction at school. Students should not have to do work at home for which they do not have all the prerequisite skills, adequate introduction, or background information. The student needs to be able to succeed at the task.

Homework-type activities for the most part are the primary opportunity a student has to be engaged in learning. For this reason these activities should be emphasized at school. The teacher needs the opportunity to observe and assess student performance while they are engaged in a learning activity. This is the primary, most important, form of assessment. The teacher can directly and quickly assess the quality of the match between the instructional material and the student. Observation permits the teacher to provide immediate feedback and assistance to students and prevent students from practicing errors.

Activity that follows up instruction (and currently homework is a part of this) is the work a student is most engaged in. It is the most important part of learning. It should be the focus of most assessment effort. All of this work should be at an appropriate level. Work done at school should be at the instructional level if the student is working independently under the teacher's supervision. It can even be somewhat more difficult if a student is working cooperatively within a team or with a peer tutor. In the latter case, the student is being supported with continuous feedback and support. The work, though more difficult, must still be within the readiness threshold of the student.

Homework, on the other hand, should be made up of activities that are easier. It should be at an independent level. The students should require no support and monitoring. They should be able to do all assignments with a high level of accuracy or correctness without help. Homework activities should be for practice, polish, and fluency. They should be done with accuracy, because practice must be done well to avoid practicing errors or bad habits. Students are motivated to do the work if they can do the work correctly and completely. Success and task completion are very reinforcing.

These then are the characteristics of good homework assignments: It must be work the students can readily do independently. It should be work completeable in a reasonable amount of time. It should be at an independent level of difficulty. It should be used for drill or review for fluency and mastery.

Homework should not be a substitute for follow-up activities that should be done at school. Follow-up activities are the primary engaged time for the student. Here is the opportunity to monitor student performance. The work being done here is the most important assessment opportunity. This work needs to be done in class in cooperative teams or under teacher supervision. Corrective, immediate feedback can be provided and the difficulty of the work adjusted to insure the students' success. Engaged time like this should make up a large portion of the school day. Homework cannot be used as a substitute for engaged time that must be done in class. Homework should not be another tool in the array of instruments used to make low achieving and disadvantaged students miserable.

Chapter 19

CURRENT PRACTICE
WITH INDIVIDUAL DIFFERENCES

Our present methods of dealing with individual differences in learning ability are a waste of time and resources. Why is this so? The reason is that primary attention is devoted to making students conform to curriculum standards. For example, a tenth grade student is failing biology. Any special attention given to this student will be devoted to helping him pass this biology class. He may receive supplementary help or tutoring. Someone may be permitted to read the tests to the student to bypass the student's difficulty in reading. However, the efforts will be to make the student conform, somehow, to the demands of the curriculum. Students must "toe the line" drawn by the curriculum.

Teachers may request smaller classes so they can devote more time to individual students to get them up to grade level or curriculum standards. They may request computers with remarkable varieties of software that tutor students on various subjects. These efforts do help the marginal student who can benefit from the extra explanation and repetition. He is not too far out of the tolerance limits imposed by the curriculum.

The problem with most procedures for dealing with individual differences is that they are attempts to change the student, not the curriculum for the student. For most low achieving students the curriculum must be made flexible enough to permit these students to move along it at their own pace. This is the essence of real individualized instruction.

We have a mind-set, fixed as if in concrete, concerning the correctness of the curricular lock-step. It diverts our attention from individual differences to making students conform to the lock-step. In doing so, we actually retard the progress of low achieving students.

When students don't manage to attain grade level standards even with this "individual" attention, we will then look for some defect in the student. Our efforts at attending to individual differences now move to

141

remediating or overcoming assumed defects in the student. Since the curriculum is held in such an esteemed and untouchable position, we devote all our time and resources to changing students so they will fit the curriculum.

Our attempts at individualizing instruction are procrustean. The curriculum is Procrustes's iron bed, and, like Procrustes, we make the students fit it by altering the shape of the student. These efforts are misguided. The efforts at individualization and change should be devoted to the bed and not the student.

Individualizing instruction is most importantly a function of supplying instruction of appropriate difficulty to students. This difficulty level must produce both success and achievement. Individualized instruction defined and implemented in this way is remarkably different than most definitions and practices of individualization.

Most definitions of individualized instruction have to do with numbers or student/teacher ratios. The smaller the number, the greater the individualization. The most individualization occurs one-on-one. This has become part of the basic dogma of individualized instruction for those who advocate smaller class size as the answer to improved achievement through individualization of instruction.

My view of individualized instruction has virtually nothing to do with student/teacher ratios. The match between student and the instructional level is the most important part of individualization, and it can be done without much regard to class size. However, fewer numbers of students makes the observation, preparation, and instructional time more manageable.

Unfortunately, the levels of instructional difficulty don't often vary when class size decreases. Even in tutoring situations, there may be no attempt to match the student with the appropriate level of instruction. In small classes, one level of instruction, the level assigned to that grade, will be all that each student has to use. In fact, in many tutoring situations, the level of instructional material will be higher than the achievement level of the student. The rationale for much tutoring is to get the students to work at a higher level than they are at, and rather than starting at the students' instructional level, work commences at the targetted level.

Reducing class size may be used in an attempt to make students work at one level. Since students in any classroom are actually diverse in achievement level, teachers say the only way they can make them all work at the same level is by reducing the number of students so they can better help them work at this single level. This becomes a perversion of dealing with individual differences. You are not dealing with individual differences if you are making the students work at the same grade level, even though you are spending more time working with individuals.

Some educators feel that individual students vary according to their learning style. They feel that students may prefer to learn through different sensory modalities. Individual students may prefer one from among auditory, visual, tactile, or kinesthetic learning styles. Students may be tested to determine their preference, and then teaching strategies can be developed that emphasize the strength of individual students.

Here, again, even though attention is given to some individual characteristics, the actual level of instructional difficulty is not the focus, only the perceptual format is. Typically, the results of such efforts at individualization are disappointing (Powell, 1987).

Obviously, the perceptual format of instruction has to be altered if a student has a significant visual impairment or a serious hearing loss. However, for non-handicapped students, the most important element of individualization is making the match between individual students and the instructional level of the teaching material and activities.

Curing individual differences seems to be the aim of much so-called individualized instruction. We provide individual attention, either by reducing student/teacher ratios or by designing material for a perceptual strength, in order to help students achieve to grade level norms or standards. Why is it that we resist accepting the fact that students vary in academic aptitude? It takes a convoluted logic to conclude that we can make all students perform at least up to the average of their chronological age group. We can't make all students academically similar any more than we can make children equally able musicians, artists, athletes, or mechanics. We accept variability in these aptitudes and would not attempt to make all students perform to an average level in any of these areas. We should remember the difference between normal and average. Average is a mathematical term that incorporates the entire range of levels. Normal is the total range of typical levels. Average is an abstraction; very few students would actually fit at that precise level in any class on any trait. Normal is really a wide range of ability or aptitude levels.

The problem that should be addressed is the discrepancy between aptitude and achievement that emerges when students fail. Remember, they fail when they are not given work that is at their aptitude and ability level. The solution to this problem is to adopt the form of individualized instruction that matches work with students to produce success and achievement. Forms that attempt to make students conform to standards and norms are doomed to failure. Forms that deal with perceptual preferences without teaching at individual instructional levels are also doomed.

Success must be the central concern of dealing with individual differences. It is the high performance needed in all work. Success is motivating, but it is also the central ingredient in learning. You must get correct answers in order to learn correct answers. Success is necessary to achievement.

Real individualized instruction attends to success regardless of the other arrangements. Instruction begins for students at their individual instructional levels. In all follow-up and drill activities, provisions are made to insure that they do the work well and with high accuracy. Careful monitoring of students' work is a central part of dealing with individual differences. The focus of assessment is on the material or activity. More precisely, the focus is on the match between the work and the student. If work is too difficult, then adjustments in it are made to produce success.

The method of delivery of individualized instruction is not much the issue. I have described some that included cooperative learning and peer-tutoring arrangements which have proved successful. It can be accommodated in classrooms regardless of their size. In fact, real individualized instruction becomes a very necessary arrangement when class size is large.

There are other conditions that are helpful in delivering individualized instruction. Teachers must be prepared to handle instruction on the curriculum at levels both well below and well above their specific grade. Students are actually performing years above and below as a matter of normal occurrence. One need go no further for proof than the normative data on standardized tests for each grade level to see the actual performance ranges that actually do occur. The thing teachers need is the array of instructional material for these many levels. Having only grade level material is a real hardship.

Chapter 20

A DIFFERENT MODEL OF
TEACHING AND THE TEACHER

Just as the curriculum should be student-centered, so should teaching. Teaching is not usually student-oriented, that is, focused on the ability of each of the students in a classroom. Teaching is focused on the content of the curriculum assigned to that grade or course. Lectures, activities, readings, and assignments are sequenced over the approximately 175 school days to cover the content of a course. Hopefully, teaching thus proceeds by engaging a majority of the students long enough so they make satisfactory progress. We know, however, that this method does not and cannot engage all of the diverse ability levels.

When a teacher delivers a lecture to a group of students, how much time will the students track (be engaged in) the lecture topic? No student will track the relevant lecture content during an entire 50-minute period. Lecturers must be content with about 50 to 60 percent engagement (Pollio, 1984). Now, if the student is not typical, if he is not able to comprehend the lecture presentation because of its complexity or his lack of readiness, his benefit will be nil.

The lecture model of teaching is virtually the standard. The lecture form of instruction is evaluated on subjective variables such as how stimulating or entertaining it is. Lecturing, however, is a one-level method of presentation to a group of students. Even when supplemented with various electronic media, it remains a presentation to a group.

Instruction to groups invariably misses the low achieving end of the continuum. If, on the other hand, the presentation is within the readiness threshold of all the students, then it will be inappropriate for the higher achieving members of the group.

The lecture method is teacher-centered. The teacher is certainly engaged in instruction, but the students may not be. The odds are most will not be engaged much more than half the time; the low achieving members of the group will be engaged hardly at all. However, remember the importance of engaged time to achievement. The group lecture method is a poor method of engaging students in learning.

Still, the lecture presentation is the dominant delivery system. It is probably so because it is easy to evaluate. What is going on is obvious and concrete. Teachers can be judged on their performance like an actor, comedian, or inspirationalist. The logic and clarity of the presentation (in the rater's view, not the low achieving student's) can be readily judged and judged against its curricular objectives. Control of the classroom is judged against how apparently attentive or quiet the students are as the lecture proceeds.

Discussion that occurs with or follows group lectures usually reveals the range of student engagement and comprehension. Some understand and participate. Others clearly don't. Even if the student is able to participate, the opportunity for participation is limited due to the number of students in the average classroom. The opportunity to probe, through questions, the students' level of engagement is limited in group lecture procedures. Often, the discussion and participation is carried by the more engaged, higher achieving members of the group. If the teacher tries to engage the less engaged, low achieving members similarly, it is done at the expense of the other members of the group. The pace slows and interest slackens.

Keeping students working in the range of their own instructional level is possible only when instruction becomes student-centered. Instruction is delivered according to what individuals can be engaged in and succeed in. The teachers' role in this system changes greatly. Matching instructional activities to students and selecting and preparing materials and activities takes up much of the teacher's time. The matching activities require the teacher to be constantly observing and assessing student performance in ongoing instructional activity and materials. Assessing and observing are fundamental to making the match and keeping students succeeding. The basis for identifying and preparing materials and activities are formed from the information gained from observation and assessment. These processes are a fundamental cycle that are continually tuning and matching instructional activities to students based on information gained from examining how well they perform in what they are currently doing. Instructional activity itself becomes the assessment device. Teachers use the observed results of this activity to further provide more materials and activities that are matched to individual needs.

These procedures should dominate the teacher's time. Students must be engaged; instructional decisions are based on information gained from performance while so engaged. Teachers appear to be only a participant or a member of an ensemble with the student. This contrasts with the traditional classroom where the teacher is the principle player and the students are typically just the audience.

The classroom must be well-organized to keep the students engaged at a variety of individual instructional levels. It is theoretically possible to have each individual student working independently with teacher super-vision and monitoring. However, this would take enormous care in the selection and preparation of instructional materials. Moreover, there is ample evidence that cooperative learning and peer tutoring arrange-ments are effective and improve achievement of the students involved. To make these systems work requires planning, organizational, and management skill. Much of the teacher's time is devoted to managing, supervising, observing, and measuring. Materials preparation and selec-tion takes a great deal of time in these arrangements.

Time on-task increases, and, consequently, the amount of material consumed increases much more rapidly than usual. Topping (1988) states that the rate of progress and consumption in cooperative learning programs can prove an embarrassment when it is found that the stock of available and relevant materials is exhausted.

Chapter 14 outlined cooperative learning arrangements. These arrange-ments involve the students in the actual teaching. Peer tutoring, or simply students assisting each other, is necessary and normal in a success-oriented cooperative learning environment. Teachers' time must be devoted to organizing and assisting the students in these activities.

Curriculum-based assessment is the technique that should be used to match students with instructional materials to insure that they succeed. Much teacher time is necessarily devoted to observing student perform-ance while they are engaged in learning. The teacher spends time supplying the curricular material that is used in the instruction/assessment cycle. Teachers are involved in instructional delivery, but they are not the dominating figure they are in the teacher-centered classroom. Basically, there are the two components of teaching in a system that effectively helps low achieving and disadvantaged students. They are curriculum-based assessment and some form of cooperative learning.

Curriculum-based assessment determines what instruction is to be delivered to the students. Cooperative learning arrangements provide for the actual delivery. The teachers' role is to supervise the system, select and prepare the materials, and assist and monitor instructional activity.

A considerable amount of time in each day should be devoted to planning and the preparation of instructional materials. Cooperative arrangements are necessary to give teachers this time. Assessment and observation will take even more. Assisting in and directly providing instruction take an equivalent share.

When the curriculum is not held in a lock-step and an instructional delivery system that requires a student to succeed is implemented, the amount of time devoted to materials preparation necessarily grows. When the amount of engaged time increases, the need for more material increases. Large amounts of time should be set aside for this during the school day.

The teacher in such systems appears far more managerial than pedagogical. Actually, managerial skills are needed to handle the obviously more complex organization. Managing a classroom to produce success in all the students is a complex task. However, the consequences of not doing so are often painful and demoralizing. Managing the consequences of one-level instruction in a lock-step curriculum is probably as great, but the rewards are almost nonexistent.

The teacher cannot be evaluated in the typical fashion in the system I advocate. The bulk of the teachers' time will not be devoted to things that appear pedagogical in a traditional sense. The areas where these teachers need to be evaluated focus on their students. Have the students been matched with instructional material of appropriate difficulty? Are the students successfully completing their work? Is the amount of engaged time high? Are each of the students doing as well as they can? Are the students even exceeding expectations?

In a student-centered program, the evaluation of teaching focuses on them. In a lock-step, teacher-centered system, evaluation focuses on the teacher.

The principle characteristic of a good teacher is the ability to manage the teaching at all the different instructional levels of any classroom full of students. This should be the primary component of teacher evaluation.

Chapter 14 criticized the specialist as a teacher. This was not a criticism of extensive background and skill in a subject area. It was a criticism of the isolated and provincial skill that separates small portions of the curriculum. The specialist model severely limits teachers' ability to deal with individual differences. It makes them curriculum centered and often makes them place a higher value on content than on students.

Specialization does become necessary in higher education and in advanced technical study. However, in the secondary curriculum it is a far better model to have teachers prepared to teach English, math, science, and social studies. This is simply a basic liberal arts background. Teaching all these subjects helps the teachers keep realistic expectations for the students and the assignments they give them. It helps them integrate the subject areas and permit more opportunistic teaching. More important, it lets the teacher work with fewer students over longer periods. Academically talented students might well benefit from teachers with more advanced skills in a particular area of interest, but most teachers should be prepared to teach most subjects to most children.

Small rural schools usually require teachers to instruct in several content areas and over several grades. We tend to denigrate these schools and admire larger comprehensive schools where more and more specialization occurs. We tend to think that rural schools with multigraded classrooms can't provide good learning opportunity. This is not the case. I am constantly reminded of this everytime I encounter a scientist, a physician, or scholar who has gone to such a school.

We seem to honor size and specialization. We should not, per se, honor these characteristics. Wendell Berry (1977) had some pertinent thoughts on specialists. He feels that the specialist system is a failure. Everything is done by experts, but very little is done well. Our industrial or professional products are both ingenious and shoddy at the same time.

One of the worst things about the specialist system is that it makes teachers virtually unaccountable. As specialists, the teachers are not responsible for inadequate readiness or deficiencies in the students who come to their classrooms. Those problems are for other specialists who are hired to handle these problems. The shortcomings of students are beyond consideration; teachers are responsible solely for their set of curricular objectives in their particular subject area. The inability of the students to deal with their instructional program is due to inadequacies in the students or inadequacies in the teaching by some specialist that preceded.

This type of non-specialist model is followed in Danish schools (Wham, 1987). There, a teacher will work with the same group of children for seven years. There is not the emphasis on completing a specific set of curricular objectives in a year's time. There will be more time later. Individual students can move at their own pace.

Teachers need to be given the responsibility for the achievement of all their students. This cannot be done in our specialist system. Teachers now can only be criticized on the most superficial and crudest forms of ineptitude and inadequacy. They need to be held accountable for the achievement of their students. This will only be done when teachers are responsible for students for more time, more subjects, and more levels. The relationship to their performance as teachers and the progress of their students is then unavoidably linked.

Chapter 21

A NEW PERSPECTIVE ON TESTING

Curriculum-based assessment (CBA) has emerged in recent years as an alternative to the traditional, dominant forms of assessment. As it has emerged, however, it has taken a number of different directions. This is due to different interpretations of what CBA is and to what extent some individuals tended to make this new form of assessment conform to traditional forms.

CBA is the system that I strongly advocate. It is the system needed to insure that low achieving and disadvantaged students experience success in school. However, I now find that I need to qualify what I mean by CBA. In this chapter I will briefly summarize how CBA relates to teaching low achieving and disadvantaged students. This system is fundamentally defined by Tucker (1987, 1985), Gickling and Thompson (1985), and Hargis (1987, 1982).

Much of what is presented here is a reiteration of information that was presented in previous chapters. It was integrated in many other topics. This may seem repetitive. However, since CBA is such a fundamental part of an effective method of instruction for low achieving and disadvantaged students, a summary of its essential features is presented here.

CBA is an intimate, integral part of instruction. Normal assessment procedures are isolated from teaching, while CBA incorporates it. The curriculum itself becomes the basic form for assessment. The activities that make up daily instructional processes become tests. Assessment is thus made constant and direct. It is not separate from instruction; it is fundamentally an instructional activity.

This use of instructional activity is like using the activity as an inventory. Whether reading or math, introduction or drill, student performance is monitored. The number of right and wrong are checked, or the level of comprehension is measured. The activities are themselves informal inventories. However, rather than simply marking, tallying, and scoring for the purpose of giving a grade, the information is used to see if the difficulty level of the activity is matched to the student. The number missed is checked to see if too many unfamiliar items have been introduced. If these numbers exceed the standards set for the instructional and independent levels, then the activity's difficulty is adjusted so that it does conform. This is an ongoing process. Instructional activity is constantly checked and adjusted. Scores are to be maintained in a range indicating a good match has been made.

The type of errors should be examined as well. Errors are the basis for giving helpful, corrective feedback to the students. Errors should not be merely something to be marked wrong, and certainly, students should not be given the opportunity to practice them.

Errors are of concern in CBA, but the emphasis is more on skill or what students can do. Success is a central issue, so the selection and preparation of instructional activities and materials that are doable is the necessary function of assessment information. Doable activities are made up largely of known, supportive context. Finding out what a student knows or has mastered is a major concern in CBA. This is almost the reverse of much conventional diagnostic testing. In conventional systems of diagnostic testing, one is looking specifically for skill or subskill deficiency. The focus is on deficiency. The instructional activity prescribed as a result of this kind of diagnostic testing is made up of work devoted to the missing or defective skills. Since the emphasis is almost entirely on weakness, the activities are often frustratingly difficult, and the results of such effort is often disappointing.

Success is the essential characteristic of CBA instruction, so only the number of new skills can be introduced and practiced that students can do correctly. Many activities, particularly those that require reading, must be made up largely of known words and content matter. By definition, the instructional reading level must be made up of over 95 percent known words. Sometimes, it is a major effort to find enough known words to prepare reading materials for low achieving students. Unknown words and missing skills are easy to find, and activities to present them are relatively simple to prepare, but they are unlikely to produce good results. Success is something that must be planned and structured into learning activities. This is what CBA is intended to do.

Currently, typical diagnostic tests may not represent a particular curriculum at all. CBA is made from the curriculum. It addresses the problem of test validity in a straightforward way. It insures test validity by making certain that the content of the test is made up of what is being taught.

We have assumed the validity of most diagnostic tests. However, they may have little content validity. They are unlikely to assess adequately skills presented on specific curricula. To the extent they do not measure what has been taught, they lack content validity. The problem caused by having respected, but content-invalid, diagnostic tests is that they become an additional curriculum. These tests invariably reveal skill deficits in low achieving students. Obviously, if the tests don't sample skills being taught from the curriculum being used, they will show such deficiencies. If items being measured are not taught, certainly they are more likely to be missed. However, the importance of such skill deficiencies is actually negligible. Their mistaken importance is gained from the simple fact that they appeared on a test which is imagined to have validity. Since the test is mistakenly viewed as valid, the skill deficits measured by them are viewed as significant impediments to learning. Consequently, these skills are taught; they become another curriculum. This new curriculum, made up of trivial content, will be added to the school day, taking time away from regular curricular work.

CBA requires that tests directly sample the curriculum. The best way to assure that tests have content validity is to make them up from curricular items. An aphorism of CBA is to choose tests well, for they may become the curriculum.

This leads to another dictum of CBA. It is appropriate to teach to tests. Actually, CBA is the ultimate in teaching the test. If a test is worth giving, it is worth teaching to. Why give a test if you are not going to act on the information gained from giving it. Test what you teach and teach what you test. This is how content validity is attained and how real progress is measured.

Grades and CBA do not mix. When measurement is devoted to identifying students' instructional levels and producing success, it is not possible to give a distribution of grades. The levels indicating instructional levels and success are the same for everyone. Everyone should be achieving these performance levels. To attain this state, the work provided each student must be matched to each of their ability levels. This means the difficulty levels of work must be at various levels to keep scores the same. This is the opposite of what occurs when measurement is used to give grades.

Classrooms where students receive a wide distribution of grades are classrooms where there is no real attention to individual differences in academic ability. CBA is used to attend to individual differences. When it is accomplished, such distributions of grades are not possible.

CBA forces the use of substantive reports of progress, not normative ones. Substantive reports are precise statements of where and on what students are working. They are much more useful than grades or scores. This information can be used to plot progress and to find readiness and entry levels.

CBA provides the principle procedure for the identification of learning disabilities. Low achieving students often do acquire the learning disabled label as a discrepancy emerges between their potential for achievement and their actual achievement. CBA requires that in order to be considered learning disabled, a learning problem must persist after the best match between instructional level of student and instructional difficulty has been made. This residual problem is the learning disability. The curriculum must always be ruled out as a cause first.

Failure is unfortunately our primary diagnostic tool. Using failure in this way leads to other assessment practices that are resource-draining and usually fruitless. When students fail, we seek a cause, not in the curriculum, but in the student. We often seek a deficiency in some theoretical aptitude, either perceptual or cognitive. Attention-deficit disorders are currently popular. Many tests have been created to find these various deficits. Students will be given these tests, and the areas on the test with lower scores will be considered as deficits in essential skills and therefore the cause of their failure. Treatments designed to remedy the deficit areas, or treatments designed to bypass the deficit area, will be prepared. These treatments constitute new curricula for the students. Results of such treatment programs are almost always disappointing or equivocal. The real cause of the learning problem, the curriculum, has been overlooked. This is a principle of CBA: The curriculum must first be ruled out as a cause of learning disabilities. The residual problems that persist after this is done, then, can be used as evidence of a learning problem which may then be the focus of special curricular intervention.

Finding a cause of a learning problem is important. Failure because of a mismatch with the curriculum is the most common cause, but it is unfortunately overlooked in most instances.

Chapter 22

CONCLUSION

The individual notions and ideas discussed in this book are not new, and they are not at all complex. However, when they are assembled, their composite appears radical. They appear radical because the result contrasts sharply with standard educational practice. The implementation of this system requires a radical change in some firmly institutionalized practices and attitudes.

Practices must be changed because they are the cause of most of our problems. The lock-step curriculum and its companion, the grading system, cause the vast majority of our dropouts and our learning disabled. In fact, most of the students in these two groups would be better categorized as curriculum casualties. This is a radical view.

Institutions must be changed so that we can emphasize success. All students must succeed at instructional activity. Progress is only made when students experience adequate success. Our system requires us to use a double standard. We have a standard of success for the able, those students who happen to fit the curriculum, and excessive challenge and failure for those who are less able. We must change this. Success should be required for all students. The double standard must be eliminated.

If we would assign curricula to students rather than to grade levels and courses, we could save an enormous amount of energy and resources. Trying to make students conform to grade level standards requires much effort and so does dealing with the array of problems that result from the attempt. We may think that the change would be expensive and require even more effort. Actually, the effort and expense is markedly less. There will need to be many fewer special programs for students and many fewer administrative personnel involved in managing these programs, qualifying students for them, and dealing with the behavioral consequences of failure.

When students are expected to succeed, there is no need to isolate them from their fellow students. Cooperative, rather than competitive, organizations should be introduced. These arrangements increase the students' academically engaged time and improve the quality of follow-up and drill activities. They permit teachers to have more time to observe students and prepare instructional activities that match student ability.

Students need to be more engaged in learning and instruction. There are a variety of cooperative learning arrangements that have been described that do permit this. The multigrade rural school model encourages cooperative learning and peer-tutoring activities. In single grade classrooms, cooperative learning has demonstrated its effectiveness. Cooperative teams of students do work together with significant increases in achievement.

A standard of success requires high performance on all activities. When students are supposed to do well and they are in a cooperative rather than a competitive environment, cheating is no longer a significant issue. Students are supposed to help each other do the best work they can. Classroom organization is such that this help is encouraged.

When the standard of success is adopted, grading systems must be abandoned. Assessment of achievement will be conducted with valid, substantive measures. Actual achievement is increased when students work at their individual instructional levels. If they are working at these levels, the indicators of this performance will be the same, but the instructional levels will be quite varied.

In schools where grades are highly valued and where wide distributions of grades are given, individual differences are not honored. Low achieving and disadvantaged students suffer greatly in such environments. When schools deal with individual differences adequately, the assignment of conventional grades will be impossible. Evaluation efforts will focus on the substantive measure of achievement and the assessment of daily instructional activity to assure that it is matched to student ability. Assessment should not be used to give grades to students. A distribution of grades in a classroom is actually a measure of the extent to which a teacher does not deal with individual differences.

Grades help justify assigning curricula to grade levels rather than to students. Grades permit us to blame students for lack of achievement. A student's poor performance is the student's problem, not the school's.

Even though grades have no redeeming features, they are an institution. They will be very difficult to eliminate or even modify.

The effective instruction of the multiple ability levels that exists in any classroom requires a different model of teaching than we currently have. Actually, we are in a quandary over what the characteristics of a good teacher are. We actually make it impossible for teachers to be truly effective, and this is certainly true for their low achieving students. When we make teachers perform within a lock-step, it prevents them from being effective with the full range of students. The most essential characteristic of effective teachers is their ability to provide for individual differences in their classrooms. By this I mean how well they match the instructional material and activity to the instructional level of students.

Evidence of such effectiveness is shown in increased time engaged in learning by students and the high performance levels of their routine work. Teachers are not obvious performers in such situations. Their skills are more in organization, management, and material selection and preparation.

Some school organizations will encourage dealing with individual differences. Any organizational system that breaks down the lock-step is to be encouraged. Schools should not start at the same time for all students each year. Students should be able to enter school at the time of the year that they demonstrate readiness. They should also be able to move to the next grade or level anytime during the year. Kindergarten should be open-ended and its curricula should be flexible enough to manage preschool to academic readiness levels. It should not be thought of as a nine-month period. A child's time spent in kindergarten should be permitted to range from just a few months to more than two years.

Teachers should be permitted to stay with the same students for longer periods and should be able to move up the curriculum with their students. Teachers should be permitted to work cooperatively over the grade levels, or they should themselves cover primary, intermediate, or secondary grades. This permits teachers to stay in contact with students for longer periods; it permits them to pool talent, time, and teaching resources.

Teaching materials should not be assigned to rooms by single grade levels. Neither should a single level of curricular objectives be assigned to a classroom. A range of grade levels of materials and curricular objectives that reflect the actual range of instructional levels that exist in the room should be assigned to each teacher and each room. Materials and curriculum should be assigned to children, not to rooms or grades. Curriculum should conform to children, not the reverse.

Report cards should become substantive reports of achievement. They should reflect what students have learned and what they are currently working on. There should be no question about whether or not students are passing or failing; success should become the philosophical, ethical, and educational principle that guides our schools.

BIBLIOGRAPHY

Ashlock, R. B. (1986). *Error patterns in computation* (4th ed.). Columbus: Merrill.

Berry, W. (1977). *The unsettling of America: Culture and agriculture.* San Francisco: Sierra Club Books.

Betts, E. A. (1936). *The prevention and correction of reading difficulties.* Evanston: Row Peterson.

Betts, E. A. (1946). *Foundations of reading instruction.* New York: American Book.

Bloom, B. S., Madaus, G. F., and Hastings, J. T. (1981). *Evaluation to improve learning.* New York: McGraw-Hill.

Cureton, W. L. (1971). The history of grading practices. *NCME, 2,* 1–8.

Evans, F. B. (1976). What research says about grading. In S. B. Simon and J. A. Ballanca, (Eds.), *Degrading the grading myths: A primer of alternatives to grades and marks* (pp. 30–50). Washington: Association for Supervision and Curriculum Development.

Forell, E. R. (1985). The case for conservative reader placement. *The Reading Teacher, 38,* 857–862.

Gates, A. I. (1930). *Interest and ability in reading.* New York: Macmillan.

Gelzheiser, L. M. (1987). Reducing the number of students identified as learning disabled: A question of practice, philosophy, or policy? *Exceptional Children, 54,* 145–150.

Gickling, E. E. and Thompson, V. (1985). A personal view of curriculum-based assessment. *Exceptional Children, 52,* 205–218.

Glasser, W. (1971). *The effect of school failure on the life of a child.* Washington: National Association of Elementary School Principals, NEA.

Glasser, W. (1986). *Control Theory in the Classroom.* New York: Harper and Row.

Grimes, L. (1981). Learned helplessness and attribution theory: Redefining children's learning problems. *Learning Disability Quarterly, 4,* 91–100.

Hallahan, D. P., and Kauffman, J. M. (1986). *Exceptional Children* (3rd ed.). Englewood Cliffs: Prentice-Hall.

Hargis, C. H., and Yonkers-Terhaar, M. (1988). *Do Grades Cause Learning Disabilities?* Manuscript submitted for publication.

Hargis, C. H., Terhaar-Yonkers, M., Williams, P. C., and Reed, M. T. (1988). Repetition requirements for word recognition. *Journal of Reading, 31,* 320–327.

Hargis, C. H. (1987). *Curriculum based assessment: A primer.* Springfield: Thomas.

Hargis, C. H. (1985, November). *Word introduction and repetition rates.* Paper presented at the 11th Southeastern IRA regional conference, Nashville, TN.

Hargis, C. H. (1982). *Teaching reading to handicapped children.* Denver: Love.

Hargis, C. H. (1974). An analysis of the syntactic and *figurative structure of popular first grade level basal readers.* Paper presented at the 12th meeting of the Southeastern Conference on Linguistics, Washington, D.C.

Harris, A. J., and Sipay, E. R. (1975). *How to increase reading ability* (6th ed.). New York: David McKay.

Heibert E. (1983). An examination of ability groupings for reading instruction. *Reading Research Quarterly, 18,* 231–255.

Jansky, J., and de Hirsch, K. (1972). *Preventing reading failure: Prediction, diagnosis, intervention.* New York: Harper and Row.

Lofthouse, R. (1987). One man's windmill. *Teaching K-8, 17,* 39–40.

Loftus, E. F., and Suppes, P. (1972). Structural variables that determine problem-solving difficulty in computer-assisted instruction. *Journal of Educational Psychology, 63,* 531–542.

McGill-Franzen, A. (1987). Failure to learn to read: Formulating a policy problem. *Reading Research Quarterly, 22,* 475–490.

Miller, G. A. (1956). The magical number seven, plus or minus two. *Psychological Review, 63,* 81–97.

Pollio, H. R. (1984). What students think about and do in college lecture classes (Teaching-Learning Issues No. 53). Knoxville: Learning Research Center, The University of Tennessee.

Powell, L. C. (1987). *An investigation of the degree of academic achievement evidenced when third and fourth grade students are taught mathematics through selected learning styles.* Unpublished doctoral dissertation. University of Tennessee, Knoxville.

Pugach, M., and Sapon-Shevin, M. (1987). New agendas for special education policy: What the national reports haven't said. *Exceptional Children, 53,* 295–299.

Rasinski, T. V. (1988). Caring and cooperation in the reading curriculum. *The Reading Teacher, 41,* 632–634.

Resnick, L. B., and Ford, W. W. (1981). *The psychology of mathematics for instruction.* Hillsdale: Lawrence Erlbaum Associates.

Reynolds, M. C., Wang, M. C., and Walberg, H. J. (1987). The necessary restructuring of special and regular education. *Exceptional Children, 53,* 391–398.

Rosenshine, B. V., and Berliner, D. C. (1978). Academic engaged time. *British Journal of Teacher Education, 4,* 3–16.

Shannon, P. (1983). The use of commercial reading materials in American elementary schools. *Reading Research Quarterly, 19,* 68–85.

Skinner, B. F. (1972). Teaching: The arrangement of contingencies under which something is taught. In N. G. Haring and A. H. Hayden (Eds.). *Improvement of Instruction,* Seattle: Special Child.

Slavin, R. E. (1983). When does cooperative learning improve student achievement? *Psychological Bulletin, 94,* 429–445.

Slavin, R. E. (1987). A theory of school and classroom organization. *Educational Psychologist, 22,* 89–108.

Spache, G. D. (1976). *Investigating the issues of reading disabilities.* Boston: Allyn and Bacon.

Stanovich, K. E. (1986). Matthew effects in reading: Some consequences of individual differences in the acquisition of literacy. *Reading Research Quarterly, 21,* 360–407.

Stevens, R. J., Madden, N. A., Slavin, R. E., and Farnish, A. M. (1987). Cooperative integrated reading and composition: Two field experiments. *Reading Research Quarterly, 22,* 433–454.

Thurlow, M., Groden, J., Ysseldyke, J., and Algozzine, R. (1984). Student reading during reading class: The lost activity in reading instruction. *Journal of Educational Research, 77,* 267–272.

Topping, K. (1988). *The peer tutoring handbook: Promoting cooperative learning.* Beckenham, Kent: Croom Helm Ltd.

Tucker, J. A. (1985). Curriculum-based assessment: An introduction. *Exceptional Children, 52,* 199–204.

Tucker, J. A. (1987, Fall). Curriculum-based assessment is no fad. *The Collaborative Educator,* pp. 4, 10.

Uttero, D. A. (1988). Activating comprehension through cooperative learning. *The Reading Teacher, 41,* 390–395.

Wham, M. A. (1987). Learning to read the Danish way: Is there a lesson for U.S. educators? *The Reading Teacher, 41,* 138–142.

INDEX